BLACK LIVES WHITE WORLDS

Keith Ajegbo

CAMBRIDGE UNIVERSITY PRESS

Cambridge

New York   New Rochelle

Melbourne   Sydney

Published by the Press Syndicate of the University of Cambridge
The Pitt Building, Trumpington Street, Cambridge CB2 1RP
10 Stamford Road, Oakleigh, Melbourne 3166, Australia

First published 1982
Reprinted 1988

Printed in Hong Kong by Wing King Tong

British Library Cataloguing in Publication Data

Black lives, white worlds.
1. Afro-Americans in literature
2. American fiction – Afro-American authors
I. Ajegbo, Keith
813′.5408′03520396073   PS509.N4

ISBN 0 521 28463 5

Acknowledgements

The author and publisher would like to thank the following for permission
to include extracts in this anthology:
"Julilly is Sold" from *Underground to Canada* by Barbara Smucker. © 1977
by Clarke, Irwin and Company Limited. Used by permission; W. H. Allen
and Co. Ltd for "The Death of Sis Hetta" from *Jubilee* by Margaret Walker;
Mrs Ellen Wright and Jonathan Cape Ltd for "Fear" from *Native Son* by
Richard Wright; Woodie King Associates Inc. for *Frankie Mae* by Jean
Wheeler Smith and *The Convert* by Lerone Bennett Jr.; Random House Inc.,
for "Keep This Nigger Boy Running" and "The Death of Tod Clifton" from
Invisible Man by Ralph Ellison. Copyright 1952 by Ralph Ellison. Reprinted
by permission of Random House Inc.; James Baldwin for "Richard and
Elizabeth" from his book *Go Tell it on the Mountain* and for his essay *Down at
the Cross*; Granada Publishing Limited for "Olympic Gold" from *The Greatest
– My Own Story* by Muhammad Ali; Victor Gollancz Ltd for "Little Man
Grows Up" from *Roll of Thunder, Hear my Cry* © Mildred D. Taylor 1976;
Anthony Sheil Associates Ltd for *Soledad Brother; The Prison Letters of George
Jackson* introduced by Jean Genet (Jonathan Cape, 1971), copyright in the
letters © 1970 by World Entertainers Ltd; Chatto and Windus for "The
Seven Days" from *Song of Solomon* by Toni Morrison.

The author and publisher would like to thank the following for permission
to reproduce photographs:
cover picture, Sylvester Jacobs; pp. 3 and 21 Radio Times Hulton Picture
Library; p. 75 Associated Press Ltd; p. 101 Black Star.

Contents

Introduction

Slavery

The Illusion of Freedom

Escape Routes

Fighting Back

Introduction

The theme of this collection of extracts from novels and short stories is the experience of being black in American society, as seen through the eyes of some of the greatest black American writers of the twentieth century. Many of the extracts are about struggle and suffering, but they also reveal courage and triumph in the face of miserable odds. The stories transcend the particular struggle between black and white to examine man's inhumanity to man and the consequences of this to the whole human race.

The anthology is divided into four sections. The theme of the first is the experience of slavery. The second section looks at the fierce limitations imposed upon blacks after the chains of slavery had been officially removed. The writing in the third part reveals the ways in which two famous black men escaped the fate of many of their contemporaries and eventually rose to fame. The final section shows the embers of a deeply felt resentment being fuelled into the fierce flame of resistance.

I have used these selections with fourth- and fifth-year classes for a variety of reasons, the first being their literary merit and their obvious appeal. They have also been useful in theme work for "O" level and CSE English examinations, where they have added a perspective on themes such as "City Life" and "Crime". I initially became keen to put this anthology together after I had read some of the extracts at school assemblies, and a great number of pupils had asked me where they could find the books.

Keith Ajegbo

Slavery

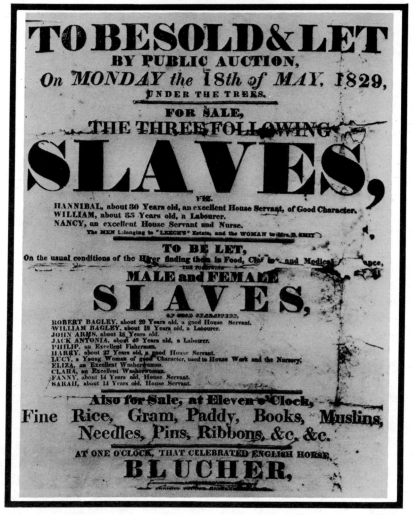

TO BE SOLD & LET
BY PUBLIC AUCTION,
On MONDAY the 18th of MAY, 1829,
UNDER THE TREES.
FOR SALE,
THE THREE FOLLOWING

SLAVES,

VIZ.

HANNIBAL, about 30 Years old, an excellent House Servant, of Good Character.
WILLIAM, about 35 Years old, a Labourer.
NANCY, an excellent House Servant and Nurse.

The MEN belonging to "LEECH'S" Estate, and the WOMAN to Mrs. D. SMIT

TO BE LET,
On the usual conditions of the Hirer finding them in Food, Clothes, and Medical nce,
THE FOLLOWING
MALE and FEMALE

SLAVES,

AS GOOD SEASONED.

ROBERT BAGLEY, about 20 Years old, a good House Servant.
WILLIAM BAGLEY, about 18 Years old, a Labourer.
JOHN ARMS, about 18 Years old.
JACK ANTONIA, about 40 Years old, a Labourer.
PHILIP, an Excellent Fisherman.
HARRY, about 27 Years old, a good House Servant.
LUCY, a Young Woman of good Character, used to House Work and the Nursery.
ELIZA, an Excellent Washerwoman.
CLARA, an Excellent Washerwoman.
FANNY, about 14 Years old, House Servant.
SARAH, about 14 Years old, House Servant.

Also for Sale, at Eleven o'Clock,
Fine Rice, Gram, Paddy, Books, Muslins,
Needles, Pins, Ribbons, &c. &c.

AT ONE O'CLOCK, THAT CELEBRATED ENGLISH HORSE,
BLUCHER,

Until they were freed by Abraham Lincoln in 1865, black people in the Southern states of America were slaves to their white masters. The horrors of slavery have been catalogued many times, revealing a terrible picture of the physical horrors that slaves underwent. In the two extracts that follow, although physical suffering is described, the emphasis is on the emotional trauma involved in being someone else's property.

Julilly is Sold

from *Underground to Canada* by Barbara Smucker, 1977

*Julilly is a young and brave girl brought up in slavery in the
nineteenth century. Her mother, Mammy Sally, worried that one
day they could be sold to different masters, has told Julilly about the
distant land of Canada. In Canada, Mammy Sally says, all people
can be free and she has heard rumours that courageous slaves have
escaped and taken refuge there.*

In this extract from Underground to Canada, *what Mammy
Sally has always feared happens; Julilly is sold to another
plantation. For Julilly this terrible experience is the beginning of a
painful journey that she determines will end in her freedom.*

Morning came to the slave quarters of Master Hensen's plantation
before there was light in the heavy, black sky. It was four o'clock
and Master Hensen's old ram horn bellowed and tooted until
nobody slept. Frying sowbelly smells from the cabin cooking fires
helped wake the children. Julilly reached for a hoecake and a tin
cup of buttermilk that Mammy Sally poured. From the barnyard the
roosters crowed sharp and clear.

As on every other morning, Julilly smoothed down her crinkly
hair and twisted it tight in a knot at the back of her head. But
Mammy Sally, who always wore a clean, white head-rag neatly tied,
this morning put on a black one in its place. There was no laughter
in her full, strong voice as she called to one slave and then another
who passed by their door. A worried frown stitched lines across her
forehead.

"Child," she said to Julilly in a yearning, mournful way, "there's
trouble ahead for us nigger folk today."

Her lips pinched firm and her eyes flamed with angry courage,
but her voice stayed quiet. She gathered Julilly's hands into the
strength of her long, black, calloused fingers.

"Lord help us," she said. "The field hands are gonna be sold
today. You are one of them, June Lilly. You and I could be pulled
apart."

Julilly couldn't understand. Mammy Sally couldn't let this
happen.

Mammy shook Julilly into listening. "If we are sold apart, June
Lilly, and the Lord forbid, don't forget that freedom land I told you

about. You and I are strong. We'll get there with the guidance of that star, and the good Lord's help.''

A jay-bird voice screeched suddenly outside their door.

''You field-hand niggers. Line yourselves up along this path and don't you loiter.'' The sound of a zinging whip cut the air. ''Some of you ain't gonna chop no cotton today.''

Mammy Sally held Julilly close as they walked outside and joined the field-hand line. The man with the jay-bird voice strode back and forth in front of them. He was a big man with a short, thick neck. His cheeks puffed and jiggled as he walked. Julilly noticed that his fingers puffed, too, over the whip that he flicked in his hand. He had a toothpick in his mouth that stuck between two yellow teeth. Julilly didn't like his oily skin. His faded brown hair was tangled and dirty, his baggy pants were streaked with drippings and his little eyes were green and sly.

He strode towards Lily Brown, a shy young mother barely sixteen. She clutched her two-year-old Willie in her arms.

The fat man paused briefly beside her. His tiny eyes narrowed and he rubbed his oily hand down Willie's bare back.

''This is a fat, strong nigger baby,'' he called to a younger white man behind him. ''Put him in the wagon.''

Willie was ripped from his mother's arms without a comment.

Lily screamed and fell to the ground.

Julilly started to run towards her, but the firm hand of Mammy Sally grasped her shoulder.

The fat man was stopping in front of them, clamping the toothpick hard between his lips. He stuck a fat finger into her mouth and squinted at her teeth. Satisfied, he pushed back her eyelids.

''Looking at me like Old John does his horse,'' Julilly thought and flamed with anger.

''This one will do,'' the big man called towards the young man who had just dumped Willie in the cart. ''She's strong and healthy and still growin'. Get over there, girl, and get into that cart.'' He strode off down the line.

Julilly didn't move. She looked at Mammy, and for the first time in her life saw fear in Mammy Sally's eyes.

''Do like he say, child.'' Mammy's voice hurt and choked. ''You got to mind that man in order to save your life. Don't forget that place I told you about.''

The fat man looked back and screeched.

''Get in that wagon, girl, or I'll use this whip and teach you how to jump.''

There was moaning now and crying up and down the line of slaves. The big slave trader didn't care or hear. He lashed his whip in the air, pulling children from their mothers and fathers and sending them to the cart.

Julilly moved towards the long, wooden cart. Her feet pulled her there somehow and she climbed inside. She looked for Mammy Sally, but Mammy was already being pushed with the older slaves far down beyond the tool shed.

Julilly strained to find Mammy's black head-rag. It was gone. Mammy Sally had disappeared!

A red sun boiled up into the sky, making patches of heat wherever it struck the uncovered earth. Julilly sat still and numb in the unshaded wagon. Little Willie Brown whimpered beside her. She wanted to comfort him, but she couldn't lift her hand. She found it hard to swallow and wondered if she could make a sound if she tried to speak.

Other children began climbing into the wagon. They were smaller than Julilly. They moved near her – their little bodies twitched like a wild bird she had caught once and held for a moment before it broke into flight.

Three men were ordered into a line behind the cart. They stood like broken trees, their hands dangling like willow branches in the wind. Julilly knew each one.

There was Ben, solid and strong and as black as midnight. He could chop a woodpile higher than his head when the others still had little mounds up to their knees.

There was kind, gentle Adam whose singing was low as the sightless hollow of a tree. And then there was Lester, the mulatto with speckly skin and angry eyes. Each one had a wife and one or two babies. They didn't move when the fat man with his puffed, oily fingers clamped a chain around their legs.

Julilly watched. The chain became a silver snake. It coiled over the ground, around the men, and up onto the back of their cart. It bit into a lock that held it fast.

Another strange white man led a work-horse in front of them. Julilly was afraid to look at him. She felt the tug and jerk of the wagon and the bounce of the man as he jumped onto the front seat.

"Gid-eee-up," he cried, snapping the reins.

The snake-chain jingled in protest while the men, who were not used to it, tried to swing their bound legs in some sort of order. The fat man, with the toothpick still in his mouth, rode behind them on a smooth brown horse.

They moved down the dusty road, past the empty slave cabins and around by Master Hensen's house. It was empty. There were no curtains in the tall windows or chairs on the wide, shaded porch. Massa and Missy Hensen were gone.

Old John came through the wide front door, hobbled and bent. He shaded his eyes to watch the chain gang and the wagon load of children. When he saw Julilly, his back straightened. Pulling a large, white handkerchief from his pocket, he waved it up and down – up and down – up and down – until it became a tiny speck and disappeared.

Tears ran down Julilly's cheeks. She couldn't stop them, but she made no sound. The fat man didn't notice her.

Follow-up

1   In this extract what do you learn about the character of Mammy Sally?
2   Imagine that you are Mammy Sally. Write down all the thoughts and feelings that are racing through your head as that wagon takes Julilly away.
3   Describe the appearance of the man with "the jay-bird voice". Imagine he is telling his wife about buying Julilly and the other slaves. Write down what you think he would say.

The Death of Sis Hetta

from *Jubilee* by Margaret Walker, 1966

This extract is from the novel Jubilee *which follows the life of Vyry, a woman who is born in slavery and lives through the great political and social upheavals in America, during the latter part of the nineteenth century. Vyry suffers the humiliations and pain of slavery, the uprooting of the American Civil War and all the disappointments that followed in the wake of the Emancipation of Slaves in 1865. Although this is a story of much sadness and suffering, it is also a story of determination, hope and triumph. It is, in fact, based on the true history of Margaret Walker's great-grandmother, who, she writes, "is the Vyry of this story".*

This extract is the first chapter of the book; it describes the tragic death of Vyry's mother, Sis Hetta, in childbirth. The description provides a sensitive insight into the complicated relationships that existed between black people and white people in the slave plantation.

"May Liza, how come you so restless and uneasy? You must be restless in your mind."

"I is. I is. That old screech owl is making me nervous."

"Wellum, 'tain't no use in your gitting so upset bout that bird hollering. It ain't the sign of no woman nohow. It always means a man."

"It's the sign of death."

Grandpa Tom, the stable boy, and May Liza, Marster's upstairs house girl, were sitting on the steps of their cabins in the slave Quarters. It was not yet dusk-dark. An early twilight hung over the valley, and along the creek bank fog rose. The hot spring day was ending with the promise of a long and miserable night. A hushed quiet hung over the Quarters. There were no children playing ring games before the cabins. The hardened dirt-clay road, more like a narrow path before their doors, was full of people smoking corncob pipes and chewing tobacco in silence. Out on the horizon a full moon was rising. All eyes were on the cabin of Sis Hetta, where she lay on her deathbed sinking fast.

Inside Sis Hetta's cabin the night was sticky hot. A cloying, sweetish, almost sickening smell of Cape jessamine, honeysuckle, and magnolias clung heavily to the humid night air. Caline, a middle-aged brown-skin woman with a head of crinkly brown hair tied in a knot on her neck, imposing eyes, and the unruffled air of importance and dignity that one associated with house servants, stood beside the sickbed and fanned Sis Hetta with a large palmetto fan. Caline knew Hetta was dying. As soon as supper was over in the Big House, Caline came to see what she could do. Aunt Sally, cook in the Big House, couldn't get away with Caline but she sent word, "Tell em I'll be along terreckly." Fanning Sis Hetta in the hot night seemed all there was left to do for her, and so Caline kept fanning and thinking: Sis Hetta was a right young woman, younger than Caline, and she got with all those younguns fast as she could breed them. Caline had no children. She had never known why.

Maybe it was something Old Marster made them do to her when she was a young girl and first started working in the Big House. Maybe it was the saltpetre. Anyway, Caline was glad. Slaves were better off, like herself, when they had no children to be sold away, to die, and to keep on having till they killed you, like Hetta was dying now.

Out on the Big Road, May Liza and Grandpa Tom could barely discern a man in the distance. As he drew nearer they could see he was riding a small child on his shoulders.

"Brother Zeke," breathed May Liza.

"Yeah," and Grandpa Tom took his pipe out of his mouth and spat.

"That's Sis Hetta's last child she had for Marster, Zeke's riding on his shoulder."

"How you know?"

"I hear tell they done sent clean over to Marster's other plantation cause Hetta wants to look at her youngun."

"Be her last look, I reckon."

"Yeah, I reckon so."

Now in the tricky light of the half-night they saw a figure wearing long trailing skirts of a woman. She was walking slowly at a short distance behind Brother Ezekiel.

"Mammy Sukey's coming too."

"You know she ain't leaving that gal out of her sight. That's Marster's youngun they give her to raise."

"Marster don't care nothing bout that youngun. Mammy Sukey's got her cause Jake won't leave her be in peace with him and Hetta. They say he pinch that gal when she wasn't nothing but a suckling baby."

"Wellum 'twarn't no use in that. Jake knowed Hetta been having Marster's younguns long as they can remember."

"Reckon how he knowed?"

Hetta was twenty-nine years old, although this was a fact she could not verify. After having given birth to fifteen children, all single births, she was waiting for death in childbed. Her thin bony fingers clutched nervously at the ragged quilt that covered her. Evidently her mind wandered back over happier and earlier days, for her quick beady eyes, glittering with fever, sometimes lighted up, and although she was nearly speechless, Caline fancied she heard the sick woman muttering words. Hetta was a woman who had never talked much.

Another black woman, small, and birdlike in her movements,

moved in and out the cabin carrying china washbowls and pitchers of hot water; moving blood-soaked rags and clothing, watching the face of the sick woman to whom she had fed laudanum to ease the pain of these last three days. Granny Ticey was deeply dejected. She moved to keep her hands busy and occupy her mind. She had always been proud of her reputation of rarely losing her patients. Babies she lost, but mothers seldom. She had been uneasy all week about Hetta. It wasn't the first time this heavy breeding woman, whose babies came too fast, tearing her flesh in shreds, had had a hard and complicated time. She did not like either the looks or the actions of Hetta and she told Jake and Marster, or at least tried to communicate her fears to them. Of course it was true there wasn't anything too much she had to base her fear on. Hetta was sick every day this last time. Toward the end she rarely left her bed. She was bloated and swollen beyond recognition. But Jake said nothing, as usual, and Marster only laughed. Eight days ago when Granny Ticey saw the quarter moon dripping blood she knew it was an evil omen. When Jake came for her and said Hetta's time had come she did not want to go, because she knew nothing was right. But she went and she stayed, and now grim and wordless she watched the night lengthen its shadows outside Sis Hetta's door.

One thing Granny Ticey had done. When the baby was born dead, and Hetta started having terrible fits and haemorrhaging, she made Marster send for a doctor, but two days went by before the doctor came. Meanwhile Granny Ticey made tansy tea and bathed Hetta in hazel root, and used red shank. All these did no good. On the third day when the white doctor came, he barely stayed ten minutes, and he did not touch Hetta. Instead he spoke angrily to Granny Ticey.

"What you want me to do, now that it's plain she's dying? You didn't get all that afterbirth. How many times do I have to tell you to get it all? Don't know why you had John to get me way out here for this unless it was just to make him waste money over your carelessness."

Granny Ticey said nothing. Her lips were tight and her eyes were hard and angry in an otherwise set face. But she was thinking all she dared not say: How was he expecting me to get all the rotten pieces after a dead baby? That's exactly why I sent for him, so's he could get what I couldn't get. If he had come on when I sent for him, instead of waiting till now, Hetta might not be dead. No, I'll take that back. She was going to die anyway. She had to die one of these times. The last two times were nothing but the goodness of God. I guess it's just her time.

When the doctor went away he must have told Marster that Hetta was dying. Early in the afternoon when dinner in the Big House was over, Marster came down to Hetta's cabin. Granny Ticey was there alone with Hetta. Jake was in the fields. Marster was a tall blond man barely thirty-five years old. John Morris Dutton scarcely looked like the Marster. He still looked like a boy to Granny Ticey, but a big husky boy, whose sandy hair fell in his face and whose grey-blue eyes always twinkled in fun. He liked to hunt and fish, and he was always slapping a friend on the back in good fellowship and fun. He never seemed to take anything too seriously, and his every other word was a swearing, cursing song. He was a rich man with two plantations and sixty slaves on this one. He was a young man with hot blood in his veins. He could eat and drink as much as he liked, sleep it off quickly, rise early ready to ride far and enjoy living. Now he came down the path whistling, and only when his rangy form stooped to enter Hetta's cabin, and he saw the disapproving gravity in Granny Ticey's solemn eyes, did he hush, and ask, unnecessarily, "Where is she?"

Granny Ticey pointed behind the heavy quilt hanging from top to bottom of the cabin and separating the cooking corner of the fireplace and iron pots from the place where Hetta slept. Marse John pushed the quilt aside and stood over Hetta. A foetid odour made him sick for a moment, but he saw her eyes looking at him, and he called her name . . .

"Hetta?"

"Yassah." Her voice was so weak and soft he bent lower over her.

"Hetta, do you know me?"

"Yassah, Marster, I knows you." But her voice was only a whisper.

"How you feeling?"

"Poorly Marster, mighty poorly."

"I'm sorry. Is there anything you want? Something I can do for you?"

"Nossah, Marster, nothing nobody can do now. Hetta ain't long for this world."

"Oh, shut up! You're going to get well in a jiffy; be up and around in no time, as usual. You just feel bad cause you've had a bad time."

"Nossah, that ain't it. I'm dying, Marster, and I knows it. Just one thing I wanta . . ."

"What's that?"

"I wants to see my youngun Vyry, fore I dies."

"I'll send for her. Now you lay still and get well. I'll be back to see you tomorrow." And he patted her hand and went outside. But when he went out he was not gay. He thought, "By God, she might be dying at that!"

And he began to think through the years when Hetta was a young girl and there was no thought of her dying, ever. His father gave him Hetta when he was still in his teens and she was barely more than a pickaninny. He remembered how she had looked growing up, long legged like a wild colt and just that temperamental. She looked like some African queen from the Congo. She had a long thin neck and she held her head high. She must have imagined herself, he thought, in an African jungle among palms and waterfalls with gold rings coiled around her neck. Her small young breasts tilted up, and even her slight hips and little buttocks were set high on her body. When she moved lightly and they switched lazily and delicately, they titillated him and his furious excitement grew while watching her walk. It was all his father's fault. Anyway it was his father who taught him it was better for a young man of quality to learn life by breaking in a young nigger wench than it was for him to spoil a pure white virgin girl. And he had wanted Hetta, so his father gave her to him, and he had satisfied his lust with her. Because in the beginning that was all he had felt, a youthful lust. He still remembered her tears, and her frightened eyes, and how she had pleaded to be left alone, but he had persisted until she had given in to him. And things went along like that for a good while, until he began to think about getting married. At least his father thought about it first. His father kept pestering him to find a lovely young lady and make her his wife. It was time he assumed his responsibilities and settled down. So he went travelling and hunting for a wife. Between courting times he came back to Hetta. At home he took her as a matter of course, but when he went away he thought about her and he could see her and feel her and smell the musklike odour of her body in his mind. Clean enough to bathe twice a day and quiet enough never to annoy him with chatter, she provided him with all the physical release he needed. When she began having babies it was no problem. He gave her Jake for a husband and that was that.

But finally he found a wife, a beautiful young lady of quality from a fine old family in Savannah. And he married Salina. He was sure that she was madly in love with him, and when she kissed him demurely and let him hold her hand he felt sure there was enough fire in this pretty brunette girl to excite him forever. There was an elaborate wedding. He still remembered the drinking, and Salina's mother crying because her daughter was leaving home for the first time and going into the backwoods of Georgia. He could still see Salina's father grasping John Morris Dutton's hand and getting all choked up, and begging him in a voice hoarse with drink as much as anything else, "Boy, take care of my little Salina." Salina wasn't little. She was a big-boned girl, tall, and inclined to get fat. And John Morris got all emotional himself. Incoherently he promised, no, vowed like a knight on a charger to protect her with his life and to be good to her all the days of his life. Then they rode away in a buggy amidst a shower of rice, Salina laughing and crying, and John Morris Dutton just a wee bit tight.

They had a long journey, and a new house waiting, and he could understand why his wedding night was not a night of love, why she begged off with fatigue. What he never understood was why Salina acted outraged and shocked when he finally made love to her. She was pious and romantic and she locked her door most nights against him. When she finally became pregnant and suffered morning sickness his hopes ended. He went back to Hetta.

Everything was the same for a long time after that. Salina made him understand that sex, to her mind, was only a necessary evil for the sake of procreation. When she had presented him with a son and a daughter, she further informed him that her duty as a wife had ended. She simply would not, no, she simply could not go through all that suffering again. She did not want any more children, and consequently there was no more need for sex. At first he was stunned. He got drunk and got up nerve enough to tell her a few pointed facts, but beyond a few curse words nothing prevailed over her tears. His next shock came when she found out about Hetta. She pitched a lovely tantrum then. She threw things at him, called him a beast, cried three days in a row, and even packed to go home to mother. But when he encouraged her to go, offered to pay all her expenses there and continue to provide for her after she got home, only leave his children with him, she relented. Although she never forgave him, she never left him. Miscegenation was no sin to Marse John. It was an accepted fact of his world. What he could not understand at first was where Salina had been given such romantic notions, and how her loving parents had kept the facts of life from her.

Now, Hetta was dying. He would miss her. Perhaps Salina will be pleased, he thought, except for the child. With a sudden jolt, he remembered Vyry.

Vyry was two years old. Mammy Sukey had been keeping her as

she kept all Marster's bastards till they were big enough to work. She and Brother Ezekiel had nearly a two-mile walk bringing Vyry to see her dying mother, Hetta.

Brother Ezekiel was a powerfully built, stovepipe-black man. He was neither young nor old. He was the plantation preacher, at least among the slaves. He could read and write, but the white folks did not know this. Now as he came along with Vyry on his shoulders, and Mammy Sukey walking behind, he was humming a song:

> Soon one morning,
> Death come knockin at my door . . .

When they got to Sis Hetta's cabin door Aunt Sally met them. She was still in her voluminous apron, had her head-rag on, and she went inside with them.

Jake was sitting inside with a little black girl on his knees. Her eyes looked big as saucers in her thin face, and she had her thumb and two fingers in her mouth sucking on all three hard as she could.

Granny Ticey, Aunt Sally, Brother Ezekiel with Vyry in his arms, and Mammy Sukey all stood around Hetta's bed. Jake had not moved from his corner, but he sat where he could look behind the quilt. Granny Ticey spoke first.

"Hetta! Hetta! Here's Brother Zeke with Vyry. He done brung your youngun to you."

But the sick woman seemed in a stupor and hard to arouse. Brother Ezekiel moved forward while Aunt Sally and Caline stood on both sides of the bed, and while Granny Ticey propped Hetta's head higher the other two women lifted her up just as Brother Ezekiel held the child down over her and spoke, afar, "Sis Hetta, here is Vyry."

Mammy Sukey stood aside, a wizened old crone with a red rag on her head and her arms akimbo. Now the urgency in Brother Ezekiel's voice seemed to rouse the dying woman. Her eyes flickered, and her lips moved. She put up her bony hands and fluttered them like a bird. A scarcely audible and muffled sound came from her lips. Then with great effort she spoke, raspy and indistinct, but clear enough for them to know she was saying, "Vyry?"

Brother Ezekiel held the child down close to her mother's face and said, soothingly, "It's your mama, Vyry, say hello to your maw." The child spoke, "Mama," and then she whimpered. Hetta fell back on her pillows and Ezekiel handed the child to Mammy Sukey, who quickly took her outside into the night air.

After a moment Brother Ezekiel spoke again to the dying and exhausted woman.

"Sis Hetta, I'm here, Brother Zeke, it's me. Can I do something for you?"

"Pray," she rasped, "pray."

He fell on his knees beside the bed and took her hand in his. The night was growing darker. Despite the full moon outside, spilling light through the great oak and magnolia trees, inside Granny Ticey had lighted a large tallow candle. It flared up suddenly, and eerie shadows searched the corners and crowded the room. Brother Ezekiel began to pray:

"Lord, God-a-mighty, you done told us in your Word to seek and we shall find; knock and the door be open; ask, and it shall be given when your love come twinklin down. And Lord, tonight we is a-seekin. Way down here in this here rain-washed world, kneelin here by this bed of affliction pain, your humble servant is a-knockin, and askin for your lovin mercy, and your tender love. This here sister is tired a-sufferin, Lord, and she wants to come on home. We ask you to roll down that sweet chariot right here by her bed, just like you done for Lishy, so she can step in kinda easy like and ride on home to glory. Gather her in your bosom like you done Father Abraham and give her rest. She weak, Lord, and she weary, but her eyes is a-fixin for to light on them golden streets of glory and them pearly gates of God. She beggin for to set at your welcome table and feast on milk and honey. She wants to put on them angel wings and wear that crown and them pretty little golden slippers. She done been broke like a straw in the wind and she ain't got no strength, but she got the faith, Lord, and she got the promise of your Almighty Word. Lead her through this wilderness of sin and tribulation. Give her grace to stand by the river of Jordan and cross her over to hear Gabe blow that horn. Take her home, Lord God, take her home."

And the sobbing women listening to him pray breathed fervent amens. When Brother Ezekiel got up from his knees he put the hand of Sis Hetta on her cover. But she no longer seemed to hear what he was saying. Her eyes were fixed and staring above her, and her throat made raspy noises. Brother Ezekiel went outside and sat in the dampening night air. Caline got a dipper of well water and with a clean rag began to drop water in Hetta's mouth and moisten her throat. But the water trickled out of the side of her mouth and ran down her chin, and the noises in her throat grew more raspy.

Jake got up to lay his black baby on a pallet, and then with a terrible groan he walked outside where the friends of Hetta sat waiting for her to die.

A few yards from the cabin Granny Ticey had built a fire under a big, black iron wash pot. Pine knots and hickory wood sputtered and burned with sudden spurts of bright flame, emitting an aromatic smoke and discouraging mosquitos and even the lightning bugs. At odd intervals Granny Ticey threw something in the pot and something on the fire. Each time a hissing noise of water boiling over the flames, and fresh knots catching fire flared up, it startled the watchers. When the flames flared they lighted the faces of the slaves sitting watch, and when the pot boiled over they jumped in fear and suspense.

Jake did not feel sociable. He wanted to go off alone in the woods or work in the fields and not be here when Hetta died. Whenever her eyes closed in death, his fate would be sealed. Marster would have no further use for him and he would be sold. Maybe not right away, but sooner or later, it would happen after awhile. What would they do with his helpless black child then?

Hetta had been a good wife to him. He remembered how she kicked and screamed first time he "knocked her up" and he remembered the bitter dry taste in his mouth when he realized she was Marster's woman. Marster had broke her in, and then "give her to me." She kept the cabin clean and she cooked good greens and corn pone. She never went to the fields and she always smelled clean. She made him bathe every day when he came from the fields and she never showed him her nakedness, but she never refused him either. Often when he found her crying after Marster's visits while he, Jake, was in the fields he would get mad, but she never would talk except to keep him from doing foolish things. When their children were sold away and some babies never cried she would cry and grieve over their helplessness. She was a sullen-looking woman with a pouting lip who rarely smiled and almost never talked and who kept her hair wrapped in endless clean little rags. Once, when she was young and shapely, she was proud and she walked like she owned the earth. He felt sometimes because she was Marster's woman that maybe she thought herself too good for him, but she never said so, and no, she never acted that way either. But maybe it was just an evil thought in his mind anyway.

Jake's path seldom crossed Marster's. He stayed out of his way as much as possible, but if by chance they ever came face to face, Marster laughed and slapped Jake's back and talked down to his

slave, Jake, like he did to one of his good hound dogs. Jake hated
Marster and despised himself and looked at Hetta and got mad and
evil. But that was the end of it. He never dared say anything or do
anything about it.

   Now she was no longer young and slender and lovely. Her breasts
were long and flabby; her belly always bloated, whether she was big
in family way or not, and her legs and thighs were now covered
with large broken blood vessels that made it painful when she stood
long or walked far. Only her black face was still the same, serene,
dignified, sullen, and quiet by turns. Even her neck was changed
and looked shorter. Her hair was still the same, and her hands and
feet were still small, and she still believed in everything being
spotlessly clean.

   "Well, now she is dying, and they'll send me away. I guess in a way
I ought to be glad. Guess in a way I am glad to get away from here.
Marster's always said he'll get a fair price for a good stud like me."

   Midnight came and thirteen people waited for death. The black pot
boiled, and the full moon rode the clouds high in the heavens and
straight up over their heads. The child, Vyry, stirred in the arms of
her nurse, the old black crone, Mammy Sukey. Aunt Sally, sitting
near Tom and May Liza, had made a place for her son, Sam, the
carriage boy, to sit beside her. It was not a night for people to sleep
easy. Every now and then the squinch owl hollered and the
crackling fire would flare and the black pot boil. Aunt Sally kept
wondering what would happen to the little girl, Vyry, not only now,
but when she got too big for Mammy Sukey to keep her. Would
Marster bring her in his house as he had done all his other bastards?
Even though they never lasted long in the Big House, what would
Big Missy Salina say? Aunt Sally looked again at the child sleeping
in Mammy Sukey's arms and thought how much she and the little
Missy Lillian in the Big House looked alike. In her mind she
thought, "They could pass for twins – same sandy hair, same grey-
blue eyes, same milk-white skin. One of them was Hetta's child, and
one of them was Big Missy Salina's. But they were both Marse
John's and there was no mistake about that. What was even more
interesting, they were nearly the same age. Granny Ticey had been
granny for both and Hetta had wet-nursed Miss Lillian just like her
own Vyry. Big Missy had been pleased as punch with her daughter's
resemblance to her father until she learned about Hetta's child and a
few weeks later had seen Vyry. Aunt Sally glanced up at the Big
House, and, just as she had suspected, the light was still burning in
Marse John's room. All the rest of the house was dark.

Sometime between midnight and dawn the night subtly began to change. Those who had been wakeful were now drugged with sleep, and those who had slept too long and hard were now wakeful. Even before the first thread of light shot like a ribbon across the tenuous line where earth touched the sky, there was a stirring of sleeping people and animals in preparation for the coming of the morning. It was four o'clock, getting-up time for the field hands, and the cocks began to crow loudly for day. In that changing hour Sis Hetta breathed her last and slipped quietly away.

It was Granny Ticey who closed Hetta's eyes. In annoyance and chagrin, and partly in genuine sadness, pity, and grief, tears rolled down her wrinkled black cheeks. With her lips tightly set, and her eyes brimming, she pulled the coarse sack sheet over Hetta's face.

Outside the cabin the watchers were half asleep, half nodding, half dozing. Now the rasping noises had ceased, and in the long, thick silence that followed they realized that Hetta was gone.

The black pot was still and the white ashes were cold. In the growing daylight the moon's wan light was lustreless on the far horizon. Soon it would be time to bathe the dead body and prepare it for an early burial, but suddenly Granny Ticey gave a blood-curdling yell, startling all the watchers and making them all sit up wide awake. She ran out of the cabin into the dawning daylight. Gathering up all her ample skirts, coarse petticoats, and apron, she threw them over her head, showing her aged nakedness while covering her face, and thus she ran blindly and screaming down the road.

In less than a minute, the death wail went up out of every cabin in the Quarters, and Brother Ezekiel began the death chant:

> Soon one morning,
> Death come knocking at my door.
> Soon one morning,
> Death come knocking at my door.
> Soon one morning,
> Death come knocking at my door.
> Oh, my Lord,
> Oh, my Lord,
> What shall I do?

Follow-up

1 From the evidence that you can find in the passage write an account of Sis Hetta's life.

2 This is the first chapter of the book and you are introduced to various characters. Write down what you think will happen in the rest of the story to Master John. Try and base your story on what you learn about his character and behaviour in this chapter.

3 Imagine that you are Brother Ezekiel. You keep a secret journal in which you are writing an account of Sis Hetta's death. Write down your feelings about her life and the way she has been treated, and what you think of Master John and of Jake and his bitterness.

The Illusion of Freedom

The short story and the extracts in this section were all written in the 1940s or later. By this time almost a century had passed since the abolition of slavery. But even if slavery had been legally abolished, the racism, implicit in the whole notion of making people of one race slaves to those of another, was embedded as deeply as ever in the consciousness of white Americans.

The blacks in these stories suffer from economic and psychological oppression that imprisons them within worlds of very limited horizons. The Boss says to Frankie Mae: "Long as you live, bitch, I'm gonna be right and you gonna be wrong. Now get your black ass outta here," and the shopkeeper says to Richard in the last story: "You black bastards . . . you're all the same." As the hero of *Invisible Man* discovers, what happens to black people is controlled by the desires of white people.

Fear

from *Native Son* by Richard Wright, 1940

Native Son is one of the most powerful and important novels by a black American writer in the twentieth century. It is set in a large northern city in the 1930s and shows the effect on a black youth, called Bigger Thomas, of the poverty and discrimination in which he is trapped. He says to his friend: ''Every time I get to thinking about me being black and they being white, me being here and they being there, I feel like something awful's going to happen to me . . .''

Because of his blackness and other people's whiteness Bigger is hurled into a nightmare of hatred and murder that finally destroys him. But while living through the nightmare, he is able to catch a glimpse of a world where people can love and respect each other.

This extract is taken from the very beginning of the book and we are drawn into a world in which at every turn Bigger's family has to battle against the humiliations of their poverty.

Brrrrrrriiiiiiiiiiiiiiiiiiinng!

An alarm clock clanged in the dark and silent room. A bed spring creaked. A woman's voice sang out impatiently:

"Bigger, shut that thing off!"

A surly grunt sounded above the tinny ring of metal. Naked feet swished dryly across the planks in the wooden floor and the clang ceased abruptly.

"Turn on the light, Bigger."

"Awright," came a sleepy mumble.

Light flooded the room and revealed a black boy standing in a narrow space between two iron beds, rubbing his eyes with the backs of his hands. From a bed to his right the woman spoke again:

"Buddy, get up from there! I got a big washing on my hands today and I want you-all out of here."

Another black boy rolled from bed and stood up. The woman also rose and stood in her nightgown.

"Turn your heads so I can dress," she said.

The two boys averted their eyes and gazed into a far corner of the room. The woman rushed out of her nightgown and put on a pair of step-ins. She turned to the bed from which she had risen and called:

"Vera! Get up from there!"

"What time is it, Ma?" asked a muffled, adolescent voice from beneath a quilt.

"Get up ffom there, I say!"

"O.K., Ma."

A brown-skinned girl in a cotton gown got up and stretched her arms above her head and yawned. Sleepily, she sat on a chair and fumbled with her stockings. The two boys kept their faces averted while their mother and sister put on enough clothes to keep them from feeling ashamed; and the mother and sister did the same while the boys dressed. Abruptly, they all paused, holding their clothes in their hands, their attention caught by a light tapping in the thinly plastered walls of the room. They forgot their conspiracy against shame and their eyes strayed apprehensively over the floor.

"There he is again, Bigger!" the woman screamed, and the tiny one-room apartment galvanized into violent action. A chair toppled as the woman, half-dressed and in her stocking feet, scrambled breathlessly upon the bed. Her two sons, barefoot, stood tense and motionless, their eyes searching anxiously under the bed and chairs. The girl ran into a corner, half-stooped and gathered the hem of her slip into both of her hands and held it tightly over her knees.

"Oh! Oh!" she wailed.

"There he goes!"

The woman pointed a shaking finger. Her eyes were round with fascinated horror.

"Where?"

"I don't see 'im!"

"Bigger, he's behind the trunk!" the girl whimpered.

"Vera!" the woman screamed. "Get up here on the bed! Don't let that thing *bite* you!"

Frantically, Vera climbed upon the bed and the woman caught hold of her. With their arms entwined about each other, the black mother and the brown daughter gazed open-mouthed at the trunk in the corner.

Bigger looked round the room wildly, then darted to a curtain and swept it aside and grabbed two heavy iron skillets from a wall above a gas stove. He whirled and called softly to his brother, his eyes glued to the trunk.

"Buddy!"

"Yeah?"

"Here; take this skillet."

"O.K."

"Now, get over by the door!"

"O.K."

Buddy crouched by the door and held the iron skillet by its handle, his arm flexed and poised. Save for the quick, deep breathing of the four people, the room was quiet. Bigger crept on tiptoe toward the trunk with the skillet clutched stiffly in his hand, his eyes dancing and watching every inch of the wooden floor in front of him. He paused and, without moving an eye or muscle, called:

"Buddy!"

"Hunh?"

"Put that box in front of the hole so he can't get out!"

"O.K."

Buddy ran to a wooden box and shoved it quickly in front of a gaping hole in the moulding and then backed again to the door, holding the skillet ready. Bigger eased to the trunk and peered behind it cautiously. He saw nothing. Carefully, he stuck out his bare foot and pushed the trunk a few inches.

"There he is!" the mother screamed again.

A huge black rat squealed and leaped at Bigger's trouser-leg and snagged it in his teeth, hanging on.

"Goddamn!" Bigger whispered fiercely, whirling and kicking out his leg with all the strength of his body. The force of his movement shook the rat loose and it sailed through the air and struck a wall. Instantly, it rolled over and leaped again. Bigger dodged and the rat landed against a table leg. With clenched teeth, Bigger held the skillet; he was afraid to hurl it, fearing that he might miss. The rat squeaked and turned and ran in a narrow circle, looking for a place to hide; it leaped again past Bigger and scurried on dry rasping feet to one side of the box and then to the other, searching for the hole. Then it turned and reared upon its hind legs.

"Hit 'im, Bigger!" Buddy shouted.

"Kill 'im!" the woman screamed.

The rat's belly pulsed with fear. Bigger advanced a step and the rat emitted a long thin song of defiance, its black beady eyes glittering, its tiny forefeet pawing the air restlessly. Bigger swung the skillet; it skidded over the floor, missing the rat, and clattered to a stop against a wall.

"Goddamn!"

The rat leaped. Bigger sprang to one side. The rat stopped under a chair and let out a furious screak. Bigger moved slowly backward toward the door.

"Gimme that skillet, Buddy," he asked quietly, not taking his eyes from the rat.

Buddy extended his hand. Bigger caught the skillet and lifted it high in the air. The rat scuttled across the floor and stopped again at the box and searched quickly for the hole; then it reared once more and bared long yellow fangs, piping shrilly, belly quivering.

Bigger aimed and let the skillet fly with a heavy grunt. There was a shattering of wood as the box caved in. The woman screamed and hid her face in her hands. Bigger tip-toed forward and peered.

"I got 'im," he muttered, his clenched teeth bared in a smile. "By God, I got 'im."

He kicked the splintered box out of the way and the flat black body of the rat lay exposed, its two long yellow tusks showing distinctly. Bigger took a shoe and pounded the rat's head, crushing it, cursing hysterically:

"You sonofa*bitch*!"

The woman on the bed sank to her knees and buried her face in the quilts and sobbed:

"Lord, Lord, have mercy . . ."

"Aw, Mama," Vera whimpered, bending to her. "Don't cry. It's dead now."

The two brothers stood over the dead rat and spoke in tones of awed admiration.

"Gee, but he's a big bastard."

"That sonofabitch could cut your throat."

"He's over a foot long."

"How in hell do they get so big?"

"Eating garbage and anything else they can get."

"Look, Bigger, there's a three-inch rip in your pant-leg."

"Yeah; he was after me, all right."

"Please, Bigger, take 'im out," Vera begged.

"Aw, don't be so scary," Buddy said.

The woman on the bed continued to sob. Bigger took a piece of newspaper and gingerly lifted the rat by its tail and held it out at arm's length.

"Bigger, take 'im out," Vera begged again.

Bigger laughed and approached the bed with the dangling rat, swinging it to and fro like a pendulum, enjoying his sister's fear.

"Bigger!" Vera gasped convulsively; she screamed and swayed and closed her eyes and fell headlong across her mother and rolled limply from the bed to the floor.

"Bigger, for God's sake!" the mother sobbed, rising and bending over Vera. "Don't do that! Throw that rat out!"

He laid the rat down and started to dress.

"Bigger, help me lift Vera to the bed," the mother said.

He paused and turned round.

"What's the matter?" he asked, feigning ignorance.

"Do what I asked you, will you, boy?"

He went to the bed and helped his mother lift Vera. Vera's eyes were closed. He turned away and finished dressing. He wrapped the rat in a newspaper and went out of the door and down the stairs and put it into a garbage can at the corner of an alley. When he returned to the room his mother was still bent over Vera, placing a wet towel upon her head. She straightened and faced him, her cheeks and eyes wet with tears and her lips with anger.

"Boy, sometimes I wonder what makes you act like you do."

"What I do now?" he demanded belligerently.

"Sometimes you act the biggest fool I ever saw."

"What you talking about?"

"You scared your sister with that rat and she *fainted*! Ain't you got no sense at *all*?"

"Aw, I didn't know she was that scary."

"Buddy!" the mother called.

"Yessum."

"Take a newspaper and spread it over that spot."

"Yessum."

Buddy opened out a newspaper and covered the smear of blood on the floor where the rat had been crushed. Bigger went to the window and stood looking out abstractedly into the street. His mother glared at his back.

"Bigger, sometimes I wonder why I birthed you," she said bitterly.

Bigger looked at her and turned away.

"Maybe you oughtn't've. Maybe you ought to left me where I was."

"You shut your sassy mouth!"

"Aw, for chrissakes!" Bigger said, lighting a cigarette.

"Buddy, pick up them skillets and put 'em in the sink," the mother said.

"Yessum."

Bigger walked across the floor and sat on the bed. His mother's eyes followed him.

"We wouldn't have to live in this garbage dump if you had any manhood in you," she said.

"Aw, don't start that again."

"How you feel, Vera?" the mother asked.

Vera raised her head and looked about the room as though expecting to see another rat.

"Oh, Mama!"

"You poor thing!"

"I couldn't help it. Bigger scared me."

"Did you hurt yourself?"

"I bumped my head."

"Here; take it easy. You'll be all right."

"How come Bigger acts that way?" Vera asked, crying again.

"He's just crazy," the mother said. "Just plain dumb black crazy."

"I'll be late for my sewing class at the Y.W.C.A," Vera said.

"Here; stretch out on the bed. You'll feel better in a little while," the mother said.

She left Vera on the bed and turned a pair of cold eyes upon Bigger.

"Suppose you wake up some morning and find your sister dead? What would you think then?" she asked. "Suppose those rats cut our veins at night when we sleep? Naw! Nothing like that ever bothers you! All you care about is your own pleasure! Even when the relief offers you a job you won't take it till they threaten to cut off your food and starve you! Bigger, honest, you the most no-countest man I ever seen in all my life!"

"You done told me that a thousand times," he said, not looking round.

"Well, I'm telling you agin! And mark my word, some of these days you going to set down and *cry*. Some of these days you going to wish you had made something out of yourself, instead of just a tramp. But it'll be too late then."

"Stop prophesying about me," he said.

"I prophesy much as I please! And if you don't like it, you can get out. We can get along without you. We can live in one room just like we living now, even with you gone," she said.

"Aw, for chrissakes!" he said, his voice filled with nervous irritation.

"You'll regret how you living some day," she went on. "If you don't stop running with that gang of yours and do right you'll end up where you never thought you would. You think I don't know what you boys is doing, but I do. And the gallows is at the end of the road you travelling, boy. Just remember that." She turned and looked at Buddy. "Throw that box outside, Buddy."

"Yessum."

There was silence. Buddy took the box out. The mother went behind the curtain to the gas stove. Vera sat up in bed and swung her feet to the floor.

"Lay back down, Vera," the mother said.

"I feel all right now, Ma. I got to go to my sewing class."

"Well, if you feel like it, set the table," the mother said, going behind the curtain again. "Lord, I get so tired of this I don't know what to do," her voice floated plaintively from behind the curtain. "All I ever do is try to make a home for you children and you don't care."

"Aw, Ma," Vera protested. "Don't say that."

"Vera sometimes I just want to lay down and quit."

"Ma, please don't say that."

"I can't last many more years, living like this."

"I'll be old enough to work soon, Ma."

"I reckon I'll be dead then. I reckon God'll call me home."

Vera went behind the curtain and Bigger heard her trying to comfort his mother. He shut their voices out of his mind. He hated his family because he knew that they were suffering and that he was powerless to help them. He knew that the moment he allowed himself to feel to its fulness how they lived, the shame and misery of their lives, he would be swept out of himself with fear and despair. So he held towards them an attitude of iron reserve; he lived with them, but behind a wall, a curtain. And toward himself he was even more exacting. He knew that the moment he allowed what his life meant to enter fully into his consciousness, he would either kill himself or someone else. So he denied himself and acted tough.

Follow-up

1 Describe the ways in which the family is humiliated.
2 What does Bigger's mother think of her elder son? Why does she call him "the most no-countest man I ever seen in all my life"?
3 The last paragraph of the extract contains some difficult ideas about Bigger's character. It ends with the two sentences: "He knew that the moment he allowed what his life meant to enter fully into his consciousness, he would either kill himself or someone else. So he denied himself and acted tough."

From these two sentences and what you have read in the rest of the extract, why do you think Bigger "acted tough"?

4   Imagine that you are Vera. Write an entry in your diary describing the rat incident, what your reactions to it were and how it affected the different members of your family.

Frankie Mae

A short story by Jean Wheeler Smith, 1968

Frankie Mae *was first printed in an American magazine* Black World *in 1968.*

Although the action of the story takes place almost a century after the emancipation of slaves, Mr White Junior holds his employees in an economic stranglehold that almost reduces them to slaves. The connection of this story with the revolutionary ideas that swept through black America in the 1960s is that it ends with mention of strikes and civil rights workers.

The sun had just started coming up when the men gathered at the gate of the White Plantation. They leaned on the fence, waiting. No one was nervous, though. They'd all been waiting a long time. A few more minutes couldn't make much difference. They surveyed the land that they were leaving, the land from which they had brought forth seas of cotton.

Old Man Brown twisted around so that he leaned sideways on the gate. Even though he was in his fifties, he was still a handsome man. Medium-sized, with reddish-brown skin. His beard set him apart from the others; it was the same mixture of black and grey as his hair, but while his hair looked like wool, the strands of his beard were long and nearly straight. He was proud of it, and even when he wasn't able to take a bath, he kept his beard neatly cut and shaped into a V.

He closed his eyes. The sun was getting too bright; it made his headache worse. Damn, he thought, I sure wouldn't be out here this early on no Monday morning if it wasn't for what we got to do today. Whisky'll sure kill you if you don't get some sleep long with it. I wasn't never just crazy 'bout doing this, anyway. Wonder what made me decide to go along?

Then he smiled to himself. 'Course. It was on account a Frankie Mae. She always getting me into something.

Frankie was his first child, born twenty-two years ago, during the war. When she was little, she had gone everywhere with him. He had a blue bicycle with a rusty wire basket in the front. He used to put Frankie Mae in the basket and ride her to town with him and to the café, and sometimes they'd go nowhere special, just riding. She'd sit sideways so that she could see what was on the road ahead and talk with him at the same time. She never bothered to hold onto the basket; she knew her daddy wouldn't let her fall. Frankie fitted so well into the basket that for a few years the Old Man thought that it was growing with her.

She was a black child, with huge green eyes that seemed to glow in the dark. From the age of four on she had a look of being full-grown. The look was in her muscular, well-defined limbs that seemed like they could do a woman's work and in her way of seeing everything around her. Most times she was alive and happy. The only thing wrong with her was that she got hurt so easy. The slightest rebuke sent her crying; the least hint of disapproval left her moody and depressed for hours. But on the other side of it was that she had a way of springing back from pain. No matter how hurt she had been, she would be her old self by the next day. The Old Man worried over her. He wanted most to cushion her life.

When Frankie reached six, she became too large to ride in the basket with him. Also he had four more children by then. So he bought a car for forty dollars. Not long afterwards he became restless. He'd heard about how you could make a lot of money over in the delta. So he decided to go over there. He packed what he could carry in one load – the children, a few chickens, and a mattress – and slipped off one night.

Two days after they left the hills, they drove up to the White Plantation in Leflore County, Mississippi. They were given a two-room house that leaned to one side and five dollars to make some groceries with for the next month.

The Old Man and his wife, Mattie, worked hard that year. Up at four-thirty and out to the field. Frankie Mae stayed behind to nurse the other children and to watch the pot that was cooking for dinner. At sundown they came back home and got ready for the next day. They did a little sweeping, snapped some beans for dinner the next day, and washed for the baby. Then they sat on the porch together for maybe a half hour.

That was the time the Old Man liked best, the half hour before bed. He and Frankie talked about what had happened during the day, and he assured her that she had done a good job keeping up the house. Then he went on about how smart she was going to be when she started school. It would be in two years, when the oldest boy was big enough to take care of the others.

One evening on the porch Frankie said, "A man from town come by today looking for our stove. You know, the short one, the one ain't got no hair. Said we was three week behind and he was gonna take it. Had a truck to take it back in, too."

The Old Man lowered his head. He was ashamed that Frankie had had to face that man by herself. No telling what he said to her. And she took everything so serious. He'd have to start teaching her how to deal with folks like that.

"What did you tell him, baby?" he asked. "He didn't hurt you none, did he?"

"No, he didn't bother me, sides looking mean. I told him I just this morning seen some money come in the mail from Uncle Ed in Chicago. And I heard my daddy say he was gonna use it to pay off the stoveman. So he said 'Well, I give y'all one more week, one more.' And he left."

The Old Man pulled Frankie to him and hugged her. "You did 'zactly right, honey." She understood. She would be able to take care of herself.

The end of their first year in the delta the Old Man and Mattie went to settle up. It was just before Christmas. When their turn came, they were called by Mr White Junior, a short fat man, with a big stomach, whose clothes were always too tight.

"Let me see, Johnnie," he said. "Here it is. You owe two hundred dollars."

The Old Man was surprised. Sounded just like he was back in the hills. He had expected things to be different over here. He had made a good crop. Should have cleared something. Well, no sense in arguing. The bossman counted out fifty dollars.

"Here's you some Christmas money," Mr White Junior said. "Pay me when you settle up next year."

The Old Man took the money to town that same day and bought himself some barrels and some pipes and a bag of chopped corn. He had made whisky in the hills, and he could make it over here, too.

You could always find somebody to buy it. Wasn't no reason he should spend all his time farming if he couldn't make nothing out of it. He and Mattie put up their barrels in the trees down by the river and set their mash to ferment.

By spring Brown had a good business going. He sold to the coloured cafés and even to some of the white ones. And folks knew they could always come to his house if they ran out. He didn't keep the whisky at the house, though. Too dangerous, it was buried down by the water. When folks came unexpected, it was up to Frankie and her brother next to her to go get the bottles. Nobody noticed children. The Old Man bought them a new red wagon for their job.

He was able to pay off his stove and to give Mattie some money every once in a while. And they ate a little better now. But still they didn't have much more than before because Brown wasn't the kind of man to save. Also he had to do a lot of drinking himself to keep up his sales. Folks didn't like to drink by themselves. When he'd start to drinking, he usually spent up or gave away whatever he had in his pocket. So they still had to work as hard as ever for Mr White Junior. Brown enjoyed selling the whisky, though, and Mattie could always go out and sell a few bottles in case of some emergency like their lights being cut off. So they kept the business going.

That spring Mr White Junior decided to take them off shares. He would pay one dollar fifty a day for chopping cotton, and he'd pay by the hundred pound for picking. The hands had no choice. They could work by the day or leave. Actually, the Old Man liked it better working by the day. Then he would have more time to see to his whisky.

Also, Mr White Junior made Brown the timekeeper over the other hands. Everybody had drunk liquor with him, and most folks liked him. He could probably keep them working better than anybody else. He did fight too much. But the hands knew that he always carried his pistol. If anybody fought him, they'd have to be trying to kill him, 'cause he'd be trying to kill them.

Brown was given a large, battered watch. So he'd know what time to stop for dinner. His job was to see that the hands made a full day in the field and that all the weeds got chopped. The job was easier than getting out there chopping, in all that sun. So Brown liked it. The only hard part was in keeping after the women whose time was about to come. He hated to see them dragging to the field, their bellies about to burst. They were supposed to keep up with the others, which was impossible. Oftentimes Mr White Junior slipped up on the work crew and found one of the big-bellied women lagging behind the others.

"Goddamit, Johnnie," he'd say, "I done told you to keep the hands together. Queenester is way behind. I don't pay good money for folks to be standing around. If she sick, she need to go home."

Sometimes the Old Man felt like defending the woman. She had done the best she could. But then he'd think, No, better leave things like they is.

"You sure right, Mr White Junior. I was just 'bout to send her home myself. Some niggers too lazy to live."

He would walk slowly across the field to the woman. "I'm sorry, Queenester. The bossman done seen you. I told you all to be looking out for him! Now you got to go. You come back tomorrow, though. He won't hardly be back in this field so soon. I try and let you make two more days this week. I know you needs the little change."

The woman would take up her hoe and start walking home. Mr White Junior didn't carry no hands except to eat dinner and to go home after the day had been made.

One day when he had carried the hands in from the field, Mr White Junior stopped the Old Man as he was climbing down from the back of the pickup truck. While the bossman talked, Brown fingered his timekeeper's watch that hung on a chain from his belt.

"Johnnie," Mr White Junior said, "it don't look right to me for you to leave a girl at home that could be working when I need all the hands I can get. And you the timekeeper, too. This cotton can't wait on you all to get ready to chop it. I want Frankie Mae out there tomorrow."

He had tried to resist. "But we getting along with what me and Mattie makes. Ain't got nothing, but we eating. I wants Frankie Mae to go to school. We can do without the few dollars she would make."

"I want my cotton chopped," White said, swinging his fat sweating body into the truck. "Get that girl down here tomorrow. Don't nobody stay in my house and don't work."

That night the Old Man dreaded the half hour on the porch. When Frankie had started school that year, she had already been two years late. And she had been so excited about going.

When the wood had been gathered and the children cleaned up, he followed Frankie onto the sloping porch. She fell to telling him about the magnificent yellow bus in which she rode to school. He sat down next to her on the step.

"Frankie Mae, I'm going to tell you something."

"What's that, Daddy? Mamma say I been slow 'bout helping 'round the house since I been going to school? I do better. Guess I lost my head."

"No, baby. That ain't it at all. You been helping your Mama fine." He stood up to face her but could not bring his eyes to the level of her bright, happy face.

"Mr White Junior stopped me today when I was getting off the truck. Say he want you to come to field till the chopping get done."

She found his eyes. "What did you say, Daddy?"

"Well, I told him you wanted to go to school, and we could do without your little money. But he say you got to go."

The child's eyes lost their brilliance. Her shoulders slumped, and she began to cry softly. Tired, the Old Man sat back down on the step. He took her hand and sat with her until long after Mattie and the other children had gone to bed.

The next morning Frankie was up first. She put on two blouses and a dress and some pants to keep off the sun and found herself a rag to tie around her head. Then she woke up her daddy and the others, scolding them for being so slow.

"We got to go get all that cotton chopped! And y'all laying round wasting good daylight. Come on."

Brown got up and threw some water on his face. He saw Frankie bustling around in her layers of clothes, looking like a little old woman, and he smiled. That's how Frankie Mae was. She'd feel real bad, terrible for a few hours, but she always snapped back. She'd be all right now.

On the way to the field he said, "Baby, I'm gonna make you the water girl. All you got to do is carry water over to them that hollers for it and keep your bucket full. You don't have to chop none lest you see Mr White Junior coming."

"No, Daddy, that's all right. The other hands'll say you was letting me off easy 'cause I'm yours. Say you taking advantage of being timekeeper. I go on and chop with the rest."

He tried to argue with her, but she wouldn't let him give her the water bucket. Finally he put her next to Mattie so she could learn from her. As he watched over the field, he set himself not to think about his child inhaling the cotton dust and insecticide. When his eyes happened on her and Mattie, their backs bent way over, he quickly averted them. Once, when he jerked his eyes away, he found instead the bright yellow school bus bouncing along the road.

Frankie learned quickly how to chop the cotton, and sometimes she even seemed to enjoy herself. Often the choppers would go to the store to buy sardines and crackers and beans for their dinner instead of going home. At the store the Old Man would eat his beans from their jagged-edge can and watch with pride as Frankie laughed and talked with everyone and made dates with the ladies to attend church on the different plantations. Every Sunday Frankie had a service to go to. Sometimes, when his head wasn't bad from drinking, the Old Man went with her because he liked so much to see her enjoy herself. Those times he put a few gallons of his whisky in the back of the car just in case somebody needed them. When he and Frankie went off to church like that, they didn't usually get back till late at night. They would be done sold all the whisky and the Old Man would be talking loud about the wonderful sermon that the reverend had preached and all the souls that had come to Jesus.

That year they finished the chopping in June. It was too late to send Frankie back to school, and she couldn't go again until after the cotton had been picked. When she went back in November she had missed four months and found it hard to keep up with the children who'd been going all the time. Still, she went every day that she could. She stayed home only when she had to, when her mother was sick or when, in the cold weather, she didn't have shoes to wear.

Whenever she learned that she couldn't go to school on a particular day, she withdrew into herself for about an hour. She had a chair near the stove where she sat, and the little children knew not to bother her. After the hour she'd push back her chair and go to stirring the cotton in the bed ticks or washing the greens for dinner.

If this was possible, the Old Man loved her still more now. He saw the children of the other workers and his own children, too, get discouraged and stop going to school. They said it was too confusing; they never knew what the teacher was talking about because they'd not been there the day before or the month before. And they resented being left behind in classes with children half their size. He saw the other children get so that they wouldn't hold themselves up, wouldn't try to be clean and make folks respect them. Yet every other day Frankie managed to put on a clean starched dress, and she kept at her lessons.

By the time Frankie was thirteen she could figure as well as the preacher, and she was made secretary of the church.

That same year she asked her daddy if she could keep a record of what they made and what they spent.

"Sure, baby," he said. "I be proud for you to do it. We might even come out a little better this year when we settle up. I tell you what. If we get some money outta Mr White Junior this year, I'll buy you a dress for Christmas, a red one."

Frankie bought a black-and-white-speckled notebook. She put in it what they made and what they paid on their bill. After chopping time she became excited. She figured they had just about paid the bill out. What they made from picking should be theirs. She and the Old Man would sit on the porch and go over the figures and plan for Christmas. Sometimes they even talked about taking a drive up to Chicago to see Uncle Ed. Every so often he would try to hold down her excitement by reminding her that their figures had to be checked against the bossman's. Actually, he didn't expect to do much better than he'd done all the other years. But she was so proud to be using what she had learned, her numbers and all. He hated to discourage her.

Just before Christmas they went to settle up. When it came to the Old Man's turn, he trembled a little. He knew it was almost too much to hope for, that they would have money coming to them. But some of Frankie's excitement had rubbed off on him.

He motioned to her, and they went up to the table where there were several stacks of ten and twenty dollar bills, a big ledger, and a pistol. Mr White Junior sat in a brown chair, and his agent stood behind him. Brown took heart from the absolute confidence with which Frankie Mae walked next to him, and he controlled his trembling. Maybe the child was right and they had something coming to them.

"Hey there, Johnnie," Mr White Junior said, "see you brought Frankie Mae along. Fine, fine. Good to start them early. Here's you a seat."

The Old Man gave Frankie the one chair and stood beside her. The bossman rifled his papers and came out with a long narrow sheet. Brown recognized his name at the top.

"Here you are, Johnnie, y'all come out pretty good this year. Proud of you. Don't owe but $65. Since you done so good, gonna let you have $100 for Christmas."

Frankie Mae spoke up. "I been keeping a book for my daddy. And I got some different figures. Let me show you."

The room was still. Everyone, while pretending not to notice the girl, was listening intently to what she said.

Mr White Junior looked surprised, but he recovered quickly.

"Why sure. Be glad to look at your figures. You know it's easy to make a mistake. I'll show you what you done wrong."

Brown clutched her shoulder to stop her from handing over the book. But it was too late. Already she was leaning over the table, comparing her figures with those in the ledger.

"See, Mr White Junior, when we was chopping last year we made $576, and you took $320 of that to put on our bill. There. There it is on your book. And we borrowed $35 in July. There it is . . ."

The man behind the table grew red. One of his fat hands gripped the table while the other moved toward the pistol.

Frankie Mae finished. "So you see, you owe us $180 for the year."

The bossman stood up to gain the advantage of his height. He seemed about to burst. His eyes flashed around the room, and his hand clutched the pistol. He was just raising it from the table when he caught hold of himself. He took a deep breath and let go of the gun.

"Oh, yeah. I remember what happened now, Johnnie. It was that slip I gave to the doctor for Willie B. You remember, last year, 'fore chopping time. I got the bill last week. Ain't had time to put it in my book. It came to, let me think. Yeah, that was $350."

The Old Man's tension fell away from him, and he resumed his normal manner. He knew exactly what the bossman was saying. It was as he had expected, as it had always been.

"Let's go, baby," he said.

But Frankie didn't get up from the chair. For a moment she looked puzzled. Then her face cleared. She said, "Willie didn't have anything wrong with him but a broken arm. The doctor spent twenty minutes with him one time and ten minutes the other. That couldn't a cost no $350!"

The bossman's hand found the pistol again and gripped it until the knuckles were white. Brown pulled Frankie to him and put his arm around her. With his free hand he fingered his own pistol, which he always carried in his pocket. He was not afraid. But he hated the thought of shooting the man; even if he just nicked him, it would be the end for himself. He drew a line: If Mr White Junior touched him or Frankie, he would shoot. Short of that he would leave without a fight.

White spat thick, brown tobacco juice onto the floor, spattering it on the Old Man and the girl. "Nigger," he said, "I know you ain't disputing my word. Don't nobody live on my place and call me no liar. That bill was $350. You understand me?!" He stood tense, staring with hatred at the man and the girl. Everyone waited for Brown's answer. The Old Man felt Frankie's arms go 'round his waist.

"Tell him no, Daddy. We right, not him. I kept them figures all year, they got to be right." The gates of the state farm flashed through the Old Man's mind. He thought of Mattie, already sick from high blood, trying to make a living for eleven people. Frankie's arms tightened.

"Yessir," he said. "I understand."

The girl's arms dropped from him, and she started to the door. The other workers turned away to fiddle with a piece of rope to scold a child. Brown accepted the $50 that was thrown across the table to him. As he turned to follow Frankie, he heard Mr White Junior's voice, low now and with a controlled violence. "Hey you, girl. You, Frankie Mae." She stopped at the door but didn't turn around.

"Long as you live, bitch, I'm gonna be right and you gonna be wrong. Now get your black ass outta here."

Frankie stumbled out to the car and crawled onto the back seat. She cried all the way home. Brown tried to quiet her. She could still have the red dress. They'd go down to the river tomorrow and start on a new batch of whisky.

The next morning he laid in bed waiting to hear Frankie Mae moving around and fussing, waiting to know that she had snapped back to her old self. He laid there until everyone in the house had gotten up. Still he did not hear her. Finally he got up and went over to where she was balled up in the quilts.

He woke her. "Come on, baby. Time to get up. School bus be here soon."

"I ain't goin' today," she said, "got a stomach ache."

Brown sat out on the porch all day long, wishing that she would get up out the bed and struggling to understand what had happened. This time Frankie had not bounced back to her old bright-eyed self. The line that held her to this self had been stretched too taut. It had lost its tension and couldn't pull her back.

Frankie never again kept a book for her daddy. She lost interest in things such as numbers and reading. She went to school as an escape from chores but got so little of her lessons done that she was never promoted from the fourth grade to the fifth. When she was fifteen and in the fourth grade, she had her first child. After that there was no more thought of school. In the following four years she had three more children.

She sat around the house, eating and growing fat. When well

enough, she went to the field with her daddy. Her dresses were seldom ironed now. Whatever she could find to wear would do.

Still there were a few times, maybe once every three or four months, when she was lively and fresh. She'd get dressed and clean the children up and have her daddy drive them to church. On such days she'd be the first one up. She would have food on the stove before anybody else had a chance to dress. Brown would load up his trunk with his whisky, and they'd stay all day.

It was for these isolated times that the Old Man waited. They kept him believing that she would get to be all right. Until she died, he woke up every morning listening for her laughter, waiting for her to pull the covers from his feet and scold him for being lazy.

She died giving birth to her fifth child. The midwife, Esther, was good enough, but she didn't know what to do when there were complications. Brown couldn't get up but $60 of the $100 cash that you had to deposit at the county hospital. So they wouldn't let Frankie in. She bled to death on the hundred-mile drive to the charity hospital in Vicksburg.

The Old Man squinted up at the fully risen sun. The bossman was late. Should have been at the gate by now. Well, it didn't matter. Just a few more minutes and they'd be through with the place forever.

His thoughts went back to the time when the civil rights workers had first come around and they had started their meetings up at the store. They'd talked about voting and about how plantation workers should be making enough to live off. Brown and the other men had listened and talked and agreed. So they decided to ask Mr White Junior for a raise. They wanted nine dollars for their twelve-hour day.

They had asked. And he had said, Hell no. Before he'd raise them he'd lower them. So they agreed to ask him again. And if he still said no, they would go on strike.

At first Brown hadn't understood himself why he agreed to the strike. It was only this morning that he realized why: It wasn't the wages or the house that was falling down 'round him and Mattie. It was that time when he went to ask Mr White Junior about the other $40 that he needed to put Frankie in the hospital.

"Sorry, Johnnieboy," he'd said, patting Brown on the back, "but me and Miz White having a garden party today and I'm so busy. You know how women are. She want me there every minute. See me tomorrow. I'll fix you up then."

A cloud of dust rose up in front of Brown. The bossman was barrelling down the road in his pickup truck. He was mad. That was what he did when he got mad, drove his truck up and down the road fast. Brown chuckled. When they got through with him this morning, he might run that truck into the river.

Mr White Junior climbed down from the truck and made his way over to the gate. He began to give the orders for the day, who would drive the tractors, what fields would be chopped. The twelve men moved away from the fence, disdaining any support for what they were about to do.

One of the younger ones, James Lee, spoke up. "Mr White Junior, we wants to know is you gonna raise us like we asked?"

"No, goddammit. Now go on, do what I told you."

"Then," James Lee continued, "we got to go on strike from this place."

James Lee and the others left the gate and went to have a strategy meeting up at the store about what to do next.

The Old Man was a little behind the rest because he had something to give Mr White Junior. He went over to the sweat-drenched, cursing figure and handed him the scarred timekeeper's watch, the watch that had ticked away Frankie Mae's youth in the hot, endless rows of cotton.

Follow-up

1 Describe Frankie Mae's character before her confrontation with Mr White Junior over the accounts.
2 Describe her character after the confrontation and give, in detail, what you think are the reasons for the change.
   Think carefully about the sentences: "This time Frankie had not bounced back to her old bright-eyed self. The line that held her to this self had been stretched too taut. It had lost its tension and couldn't pull her back."
3 In the previous extract Bigger's mother describes her son as "the most no-countest man I ever seen in all my life." In what ways must the Old Man, Frankie Mae's father, feel of "no-count"?
4 What evidence is there in the story that things might change?
5 Write a story in which the main character is held in the power of someone else and whatever he or she does to break free only

tightens the knot. It could, for instance, be a story in which a
parent exercises a tight control over a child, or in which a
husband or wife dominates his or her partner.

Keep This Nigger Boy Running

from *Invisible Man* by Ralph Ellison, 1947

Invisible Man *is the story of a black man's journey to self-
discovery in mid-twentieth-century America. In the process of his
journey, the hero learns that, in the eyes of white America, he, as
an individual, is invisible. He travels from south to north, and his
attitude changes from a conservative desire to please and fit into
existing society to an involvement in radical politics. However, at no
point can the white people he is involved with recognize him as an
individual behind his blackness. He is imprisoned by their images of
what they believe him to be. If he steps outside the boundaries they
have laid down for him the whites will do everything in their power
to destroy him.*

*The extract, from very near the beginning of the book, provides th
young, hopeful and resilient hero with his first taste of what the
white world holds in store for him. For the respectable and
important members of the white community, he provides an outlet
for their sexual fantasies, their sadism, and their desire to patronize
and control.*

It goes a long way back, some twenty years. All my life I had been
looking for something, and everywhere I turned someone tried to
tell me what it was. I accepted their answers too, though they were
often in contradiction and even self-contradictory. I was naïve. I was
looking for myself and asking everyone except myself questions
which I, and only I, could answer. It took me a long time and much
painful boomeranging of my expectations to achieve a realization
everyone else appears to have been born with: that I am nobody
but myself. But first I had to discover that I am an invisible man!

   And yet I am no freak of nature, nor of history. I was in the cards
other things having been equal (or unequal), eighty-five years ago. I

am not ashamed of my grandparents for having been slaves. I am
only ashamed of myself for having at one time been ashamed.
About eighty-five years ago they were told that they were free,
united with others of our country in everything pertaining to the
common good, and, in everything social, separate like the fingers of
the hand. And they believed it. They exulted in it. They stayed in
their place, worked hard, and brought up my father to do the same.
But my grandfather is the one. He was an odd old guy, my
grandfather, and I am told I take after him. It was he who caused
the trouble. On his deathbed he called my father to him and said,
"Son, after I'm gone I want you to keep up the good fight. I never
told you, but our life is a war and I have been a traitor all my born
days, a spy in the enemy's country ever since I give up my gun back
in the Reconstruction. Live with your head in the lion's mouth. I
want you to overcome 'em with yeses, undermine 'em with grins,
agree 'em to death and destruction, let 'em swoller you till they
vomit or bust wide open." They thought the old man had gone out
of his mind. He had been the meekest of men. The younger children
were rushed from the room, the shades drawn and the flame of the
lamp turned so low that it sputtered on the wick like the old man's
breathing. "Learn it to the young-uns," he whispered fiercely; then
he died.

But my folks were more alarmed over his last words than over his
dying. It was as though he had not died at all, his words caused so
much anxiety. I was warned emphatically to forget what he had said
and, indeed, this is the first time it has been mentioned outside the
family circle. It had a tremendous effect upon me, however. I could
never be sure of what he meant. Grandfather had been a quiet old
man who never made any trouble, yet on his deathbed he had
called himself a traitor and a spy, and he had spoken of his
meekness as a dangerous activity. It became a constant puzzle which
lay unanswered in the back of my mind. And whenever things went
well for me I remembered my grandfather and felt guilty and
uncomfortable. It was as though I was carrying out his advice in
spite of myself. And to make it worse, everyone loved me for it. I
was praised by the most lily-white men of the town. I was
considered an example of desirable conduct – just as my grandfather
had been. And what puzzled me was that the old man had defined
it as *treachery*. When I was praised for my conduct I felt a guilt that
in some way I was doing something that was really against the
wishes of the white folks, that if they had understood they would
have desired me to act just the opposite, that I should have been

sulky and mean, and that that really would have been what they wanted, even though they were fooled and thought they wanted me to act as I did. It made me afraid that some day they would look upon me as a traitor and I would be lost. Still I was more afraid to act any other way because they didn't like that at all. The old man's words were like a curse. On my graduation day I delivered an oration in which I showed that humility was the secret, indeed, the very essence of progress. (Not that I believed this – how could I, remembering my grandfather? – I only believed that it worked.) It was a great success. Everyone praised me and I was invited to give the speech at a gathering of the town's leading white citizens. It was a triumph for our whole community.

It was in the main ballroom of the leading hotel. When I got there I discovered that it was on the occasion of a smoker, and I was told that since I was to be there anyway I might as well take part in the battle royal to be fought by some of my schoolmates as part of the entertainment. The battle royal came first.

All of the town's big shots were there in their tuxedos, wolfing down the buffet foods, drinking beer and whisky and smoking black cigars. It was a large room with a high ceiling. Chairs were arranged in neat rows around three sides of a portable boxing ring. The fourth side was clear, revealing a gleaming space of polished floor. I had some misgivings over the battle royal, by the way. Not from a distaste for fighting, but because I didn't care too much for the other fellows who were to take part. They were tough guys who seemed to have no grandfather's curse worrying their minds. No one could mistake their toughness. And besides, I suspected that fighting a battle royal might detract from the dignity of my speech. In those pre-invisible days I visualized myself as a potential Booker T. Washington. But the other fellows didn't care too much for me either, and there were nine of them. I felt superior to them in my way, and I didn't like the manner in which we were all crowded together into the servants' elevator. Nor did they like my being there. In fact, as the warmly lighted floors flashed past the elevator we had words over the fact that I, by taking part in the fight, had knocked one of their friends out of a night's work.

We were led out of the elevator through a rococo hall into an ante-room and told to get into our fighting togs. Each of us was issued a pair of boxing gloves and ushered out into the big mirrored hall, which we entered looking cautiously about us and whispering, lest we might accidentally be heard above the noise of the room. It was foggy with cigar smoke. And already the whisky was taking

effect. I was shocked to see some of the most important men of the
town quite tipsy. They were all there – bankers, lawyers, judges,
doctors, fire chiefs, teachers, merchants. Even one of the more
fashionable pastors. Something we could not see was going on up
front. A clarinet was vibrating sensuously and the men were
standing up and moving eagerly forward. We were a small tight
group, clustered together, our bare upper bodies touching and
shining with anticipatory sweat; while up front the big shots were
becoming increasingly excited over something we still could not see.
Suddenly I heard the school superintendent, who had told me to
come, yell, "Bring up the shines, gentlemen! Bring up the little
shines!"

We were rushed up to the front of the ballroom, where it smelled
even more strongly of tobacco and whisky. Then we were pushed
into place. I almost wet my pants. A sea of faces, some hostile, some
amused, ringed around us, and in the centre, facing us, stood a
magnificent blonde – stark naked. There was dead silence. I felt a
blast of cold air chill me. I tried to back away, but they were behind
me and around me. Some of the boys stood with lowered heads,
trembling. I felt a wave of irrational guilt and fear. My teeth
chattered, my skin turned to goose flesh, my knees knocked. Yet I
was strongly attracted and looked in spite of myself. Had the price of
looking been blindness, I would have looked. The hair was yellow
like that of a circus kewpie doll, the face heavily powdered and
rouged, as though to form an abstract mask, the eyes hollow and
smeared a cool blue, the colour of a baboon's butt. I felt a desire to
spit upon her as my eyes brushed slowly over her body. Her breasts
were firm and round as the domes of East Indian temples, and I
stood so close as to see the fine skin texture and beads of pearly
perspiration glistening like dew around the pink and erected buds of
her nipples. I wanted at one and the same time to run from the
room, to sink through the floor, or to go to her and cover her from
my eyes and the eyes of the others with my body; to feel the soft
thighs, to caress her and destroy her, to love her and murder her, to
hide from her, and yet to stroke where below the small American
flag tattooed upon her belly her thighs formed a capital V. I had a
notion that of all in the room she saw only me with her impersonal
eyes.

And then she began to dance, a slow sensuous movement; the
smoke of a hundred cigars clinging to her like the thinnest of veils.
She seemed like a fair bird-girl girdled in veils calling to me from
the angry surface of some grey and threatening sea. I was

transported. Then I became aware of the clarinet playing and the big shots yelling at us. Some threatened us if we looked and others if we did not. On my right I saw one boy faint. And now a man grabbed a silver pitcher from a table and stepped close as he dashed ice water upon him and stood him up and forced two of us to support him as his head hung and moans issued from his thick bluish lips. Another boy began to plead to go home. He was the largest of the group, wearing dark red fighting trunks much too small to conceal the erection which projected from him as though in answer to the insinuating low-registered moaning of the clarinet. He tried to hide himself with his boxing gloves.

And all the while the blonde continued dancing, smiling faintly at the big shots who watched her with fascination, and faintly smiling at our fear. I noticed a certain merchant who followed her hungrily, his lips loose and drooling. He was a large man who wore diamond studs in a shirtfront which swelled with the ample paunch underneath, and each time the blonde swayed her undulating hips he ran his hand through the thin hair of his bald head and, with his arms upheld, his posture clumsy like that of an intoxicated panda, wound his belly in a slow and obscene grind. This creature was completely hypnotized. The music had quickened. As the dancer flung herself about with a detached expression on her face, the men began reaching out to touch her. I could see their beefy fingers sink into the soft flesh. Some of the others tried to stop them and she began to move around the floor in graceful circles, as they gave chase, slipping and sliding over the polished floor. It was mad. Chairs went crashing, drinks were spilt, as they ran laughing and howling after her. They caught her just as she reached a door, raised her from the floor, and tossed her as college boys are tossed at a hazing, and above her red, fixed-smiling lips I saw the terror and disgust in her eyes, almost like my own terror and that which I saw in some of the other boys. As I watched they tossed her twice and her soft breasts seemed to flatten against the air and her legs flung wildly as she spun. Some of the more sober ones helped her to escape. And I started off the floor heading for the ante-room with the rest of the boys.

Some were still crying and in hysteria. But as we tried to leave we were stopped and ordered to get into the ring. There was nothing to do but what we were told. All ten of us climbed under the ropes and allowed ourselves to be blindfolded with broad bands of white cloth. One of the men seemed to feel a bit sympathetic and tried to cheer us up as we stood with our backs against the ropes. Some of us tried to grin. "See that boy over there?" one of the men said. "I want you to run across at the bell and give it to him right in the belly. If you don't get him, I'm going to get you. I don't like his looks." Each of us was told the same. The blindfolds were put on. Yet even then I had been going over my speech. In my mind each word was as bright as flame. I felt the cloth pressed into place, and frowned so that it would be loosened when I relaxed.

But now I felt a sudden fit of blind terror. I was unused to darkness. It was as though I had suddenly found myself in a dark room filled with poisonous cotton-mouths. I could hear the bleary voices yelling insistently for the battle royal to begin.

"Get going in there!"

"Let me at that big nigger!"

I strained to pick up the school superintendent's voice, as though to squeeze some security out of that slightly more familiar sound.

"Let me at those black sonsabitches!" someone yelled.

"No, Jackson, no!" another voice yelled. "Here, somebody, help me hold Jack."

"I want to get at that ginger-coloured nigger. Tear him limb from limb," the first voice yelled.

I stood against the ropes trembling. For in those days I was what they called ginger-coloured, and he sounded as though he might crunch me between his teeth like a crisp ginger cookie.

Quite a struggle was going on. Chairs were being kicked about and I could hear voices grunting as with a terrific effort. I wanted to see, to see more desperately than ever before. But the blindfold was as tight as a thick skin-puckering scab and when I raised my gloved hands to push the layers of white aside a voice yelled, "Oh, no you don't, black bastard! Leave that alone!"

"Ring the bell before Jackson kills him a coon!" someone boomed in the sudden silence. And I heard the bell clang and the sound of the feet scuffling forward.

A glove smacked against my head. I pivoted, striking out stiffly as someone went past, and felt the jar ripple along the length of my arm to my shoulder. Then it seemed as though all nine of the boys had turned upon me at once. Blows pounded me from all sides while I struck out as best I could. So many blows landed upon me that I wondered if I were not the only blindfolded fighter in the ring, or if the man called Jackson hadn't succeeded in getting me after all.

Blindfolded, I could no longer control my emotions. I had no dignity. I stumbled about like a baby or a drunken man. The smoke had become thicker and with each new blow it seemed to sear and further restrict my lungs. My saliva became like hot bitter glue. A glove connected with my head, filling my mouth with warm blood. It was everywhere. I could not tell if the moisture I felt upon my body was sweat or blood. A blow landed hard against the nape of my neck. I felt myself going over, my head hitting the floor. Streaks of blue light filled the black world behind the blindfold. I lay prone, pretending that I was knocked out, but felt myself seized by hands, and yanked to my feet. "Get going, black boy! Mix it up!" My arms were like lead, my head smarting from blows. I managed to feel my way to the ropes and held on, trying to catch my breath. A glove landed in my mid-section and I went over again, feeling as though the smoke had become a knife jabbed into my guts. Pushed this way and that by the legs milling around me, I finally pulled erect and discovered that I could see the black, sweat-washed forms weaving in the smoky-blue atmosphere like drunken dancers weaving to the rapid drum-like thuds of blows.

Everyone fought hysterically. It was complete anarchy. Everybody fought everybody else. No group fought together for long. Two, three, four fought one, then turned to fight each other, were themselves attacked. Blows landed below the belt and in the kidney, with the gloves open as well as closed, and with my eye partly opened now there was not so much terror. I moved carefully, avoiding blows, although not too many to attract attention, fighting from group to group. The boys groped about like blind, cautious crabs crouching to protect their mid-sections, their heads pulled in short against their shoulders, their arms stretched nervously before them, with their fists testing the smoke-filled air like the knobbed feelers of hypersensitive snails. In one corner I glimpsed a boy violently punching the air and heard his scream in pain as he smashed his hand against a ring post. For a second I saw him bent over holding his hand, then going down as a blow caught his unprotected head. I played one group against the other, slipping in and throwing a punch then stepping out of range while pushing the others into the mêlée to take the blows blindly aimed at me. The smoke was agonizing and there were no rounds, no bells at three-minute intervals to relieve our exhaustion. The room spun round me, a swirl of lights, smoke, sweating bodies surrounded by tense white faces. I bled from both nose and mouth, the blood spattering upon my chest.

The men kept yelling, "Slug him, black boy! Knock his guts out!" "Uppercut him! Kill him! Kill that big boy!"

Taking a fake fall, I saw a boy going down heavily beside me as though we were felled by a single blow, saw a sneaker-clad foot shoot into his groin as the two who had knocked him down stumbled upon him. I rolled out of range, feeling a twinge of nausea.

The harder we fought the more threatening the men became. And yet, I had begun to worry about my speech again. How would it go? Would they recognize my ability? What would they give me?

I was fighting automatically when suddenly I noticed that one after another of the boys was leaving the ring. I was surprised, filled with panic, as though I had been left alone with an unknown danger. Then I understood. The boys had arranged it among themselves. It was the custom for the two men left in the ring to slug it out for the winner's prize. I discovered this too late. When the bell sounded two men in tuxedos leaped into the ring and removed the blindfold. I found myself facing Tatlock, the biggest of the gang. I felt sick at my stomach. Hardly had the bell stopped ringing in my ears than it clanged again and I saw him moving swiftly towards me. Thinking of nothing else to do I hit him smash on the nose. He kept coming, bringing the rank sharp violence of stale sweat. His face was a black blank of a face, only his eyes alive – with hate of me and aglow with a feverish terror from what had happened to us all. I became anxious. I wanted to deliver my speech and he came at me as though he meant to beat it out of me. I smashed him again and again, taking his blows as they came. Then on a sudden impulse I struck him lightly and as we clinched, I whispered, "Fake like I knocked you out, you can have the prize."

"I'll break your behind," he whispered hoarsely.

"For *them*?"

"For *me*, sonofabitch!"

They were yelling for us to break it up and Tatlock spun me half around with a blow, and as a joggled camera sweeps in a reeling scene, I saw the howling red faces crouching tense beneath the cloud of blue-grey smoke. For a moment the world wavered, unravelled, flowed, then my head cleared and Tatlock bounced before me. That fluttering shadow before my eyes was his jabbing left hand. Then falling forward, my head against his damp shoulder, I whispered,

"I'll make it five dollars more."

"Go to hell!"

But his muscles relaxed a trifle beneath my pressure and I breathed, "Seven?"

"Give it to your ma," he said, ripping me beneath the heart.

And while I still held him I butted him and moved away. I felt myself bombarded with punches. I fought back with hopeless desperation. I wanted to deliver my speech more than anything else in the world, because I felt that only these men could judge truly my ability, and now this stupid clown was ruining my chances. I began fighting carefully now, moving in to punch him and out again with my greater speed. A lucky blow to his chin and I had him going too – until I heard a loud voice yell, "I got my money on the big boy."

Hearing this, I almost dropped my guard. I was confused: should I try to win against the voice out there? Would not this go against my speech, and was not this a moment for humility, for nonresistance? A blow to my head as I danced about sent my right eye popping like a jack-in-the-box and settled my dilemma. The room went red as I fell. It was a dream fall, my body languid and fastidious as to where to land, until the floor became impatient and smashed up to meet me. A moment later I came to. An hypnotic voice said FIVE emphatically. And I lay there, hazily watching a dark red spot of my own blood shaping itself into a butterfly, glistening and soaking into the soiled grey world of the canvas.

When the voice drawled TEN I was lifted up and dragged to a chair. I sat dazed. My eye pained and swelled with each throb of my pounding heart and I wondered if now I would be allowed to speak. I was wringing wet, my mouth still bleeding. We were grouped along the wall now. The other boys ignored me as they congratulated Tatlock and speculated as to how much they would be paid. One boy whimpered over his smashed hand. Looking up front, I saw attendants in white jackets rolling the portable ring away and placing a small square rug in the vacant space surrounded by chairs. Perhaps, I thought, I will stand on the rug to deliver my speech.

Then the M.C. called to us, "Come on up here boys and get your money."

We ran forward to where the men laughed and talked in their chairs, waiting. Everyone seemed friendly now.

"There it is on the rug," the man said. I saw the rug covered with coins of all dimensions and a few crumpled bills. But what excited me, scattered here and there, were the gold pieces.

"Boys, it's all yours," the man said. "You get all you grab."

"That's right, Sambo," a blond man said, winking at me confidentially.

I trembled with excitement, forgetting my pain. I would get the

gold and the bills, I thought. I would use both hands. I would throw
my body against the boys nearest me to block them from the gold.

"Get down around the rug now," the man commanded, "and
don't anyone touch it until I give the signal."

"This ought to be good," I heard.

As told, we got around the square rug on our knees. Slowly the man
raised his freckled hand as we followed it upward with our eyes.

I heard, "These niggers look like they're about to pray!"

Then, "Ready," the man said. "Go!"

I lunged for a yellow coin lying on the blue design of the carpet,
touching it and sending a surprised shriek to join those rising
around me. I tried frantically to remove my hand but could not let
go. A hot, violent force tore through my body, shaking me like a
wet rag. The rug was electrified. The hair bristled up on my head as
I shook myself free. My muscles jumped, my nerves jangled,
writhed. But I saw that this was not stopping the other boys.
Laughing in fear and embarrassment, some were holding back and
scooping up the coins knocked off by the painful contortions of the
others. The men roared above us as we struggled.

"Pick it up, goddammit, pick it up!" someone called like a bass-
voiced parrot. "Go on, get it!"

I crawled rapidly around the floor, picking up the coins, trying to
avoid the coppers and to get greenbacks and the gold. Ignoring the
shock by laughing, as I brushed the coins off quickly, I discovered
that I could contain the electricity – a contradiction, but it works.
Then the men began to push us onto the rug. Laughing
embarrassedly, we struggled out of their hands and kept after the
coins. We were all wet and slippery and hard to hold. Suddenly I
saw a boy lifted into the air, glistening with sweat like a circus seal,
and dropped, his wet back landing flush upon the charged rug,
heard him yell and saw him literally dance upon his back, his
elbows beating a frenzied tattoo upon the floor, his muscles
twitching like the flesh of a horse stung by many flies. When he
finally rolled off, his face was grey and no one stopped him when
he ran from the floor amid booming laughter.

"Get the money," the M.C. called. "That's good hard American
cash!"

And we snatched and grabbed, snatched and grabbed. I was
careful not to come too close to the rug now, and when I felt the
hot whisky breath descend upon me like a cloud of foul air I
reached out and grabbed the leg of a chair. It was occupied and I
held on desperately.

"Leggo, nigger! Leggo!"

The huge face wavered down to mine as he tried to push me free. But my body was slippery and he was too drunk. It was Mr Colcord, who owned a chain of movie houses and "entertainment palaces". Each time he grabbed me I slipped out of his hands. It became a real struggle. I feared the rug more than I did the drunk, so I held on, surprising myself for a moment by trying to topple *him* upon the rug. It was such an enormous idea that I found myself actually carrying it out. I tried not to be obvious, yet when I grabbed his leg, trying to tumble him out of the chair, he raised up roaring with laughter, and, looking at me with soberness dead in the eye, kicked me viciously in the chest. The chair leg flew out of my hand and I felt myself going and rolled. It was as though I had rolled through a bed of hot coals. It seemed a whole century would pass before I would roll free, a century in which I was seared through the deepest levels of my body to the fearful breath within me and the breath seared and heated to the point of explosion. It'll all be over in a flash, I thought as I rolled clear. It'll all be over in a flash.

But not yet, the men on the other side were waiting, red faces swollen as though from apoplexy as they bent forward in their chairs. Seeing their fingers coming towards me I rolled away as a fumbled football rolls off the receiver's fingertips, back into the coals. That time I luckily sent the rug sliding out of place and heard the coins ringing against the floor and the boys scuffling to pick them up and the M.C. calling, "All right, boys, that's all. Go get dressed and get your money."

I was limp as a dish rag. My back felt as though it had been beaten with wires.

When we had dressed the M.C. came in and gave us each five dollars, except Tatlock, who got ten for being last in the ring. Then he told us to leave. I was not to get a chance to deliver my speech, I thought. I was going out into the dim alley in despair when I was stopped and told to go back. I returned to the ballroom, where the men were pushing back their chairs and gathering in groups to talk.

The M.C. knocked on a table for quiet. "Gentlemen," he said, "we almost forgot an important part of the programme. A most serious part, gentlemen. This boy was brought here to deliver a speech which he made at his graduation yesterday . . ."

"Bravo!"

"I'm told that he is the smartest boy we've got out there in Greenwood. I'm told that he knows more big words than a pocket-sized dictionary."

Much applause and laughter.

"So now, gentlemen, I want you to give him your attention."

There was still laughter as I faced them, my mouth dry, my eye throbbing. I began slowly, but evidently my throat was tense, because they began shouting, "Louder! Louder!"

"We of the younger generation extol the wisdom of that great leader and educator," I shouted, "who first spoke these flaming words of wisdom: 'A ship lost at sea for many days suddenly sighted a friendly vessel. From the mast of the unfortunate vessel was seen a signal: "Water, water; we die of thirst!" The answer from the friendly vessel came back: "Cast down your bucket where you are." The captain of the distressed vessel, at last heeding the injunction, cast down his bucket, and it came up full of fresh sparkling water from the mouth of the Amazon River.' And like him I say, and in his words, "To those of my race who depend upon bettering their condition in a foreign land, or who underestimate the importance of cultivating friendly relations with the Southern white man, who is his next-door neighbour, I would say: 'Cast down your bucket where you are' – cast it down in making friends in every manly way of the people of all races by whom we are surrounded . . .'"

I spoke automatically and with such fervour that I did not realize that the men were still talking and laughing until my dry mouth, filling up with blood from the cut, almost strangled me. I coughed, wanting to stop and go to one of the tall brass, sand-filled spittoons to relieve myself, but a few of the men, especially the superintendent, were listening and I was afraid. So I gulped it down, blood, saliva and all, and continued. (What powers of endurance I had during those days! What enthusiasm! What a belief in the rightness of things!) I spoke even louder in spite of the pain. But still they talked and still they laughed, as though deaf with cotton in dirty ears. So I spoke with greater emotional emphasis. I closed my ears and swallowed blood until I was nauseated. The speech seemed a hundred times as long as before, but I could not leave out a single word. All had to be said, each memorized nuance considered, rendered. Nor was that all. Whenever I uttered a word of three or more syllables a group of voices would yell for me to repeat it. I used the phrase "social responsibility" and they yelled:

"What's that word you say, boy?"

"Social responsibility," I said.

"What?"

"Social . . ."

"Louder."

". . . responsibility."

"More!"

"Respon –"

"Repeat!"

"– sibility."

The room filled with the uproar of laughter until, no doubt, distracted by having to gulp down my blood, I made a mistake and yelled a phrase I had often seen denounced in newspaper editorials, heard debated in private.

"Social . . ."

"What?" they yelled.

". . . equality –"

The laughter hung smokelike in the sudden stillness. I opened my eyes, puzzled. Sounds of displeasure filled the room. The M.C. rushed forward. They shouted hostile phrases at me. But I did not understand.

A small dry moustached man in the front row blared out, "Say that slowly, son!"

"What sir?"

"What you just said!"

"Social responsibility, sir," I said.

"You weren't being smart, were you, boy?" he said, not unkindly.

"No, sir!"

"You sure that about 'equality' was a mistake?"

"Oh, yes, sir," I said. "I was swallowing blood."

"Well, you had better speak more slowly so we can understand. We mean to do right by you, but you've got to know your place at all times. All right, now, go on with your speech."

I was afraid. I wanted to leave but I wanted also to speak and I was afraid they'd snatch me down.

"Thank you, sir," I said, beginning where I had left off, and having them ignore me as before.

Yet when I finished there was a thunderous applause. I was surprised to see the superintendent come forth with a package wrapped in white tissue paper, and, gesturing for quiet, address the men.

"Gentlemen, you see that I did not overpraise this boy. He makes a good speech and some day he'll lead his people in the proper paths. And I don't have to tell you that that is important in these days and times. This is a good, smart boy, and so to encourage him in the right direction, in the name of the Board of Education I wish to present him a prize in the form of this . . ."

He paused, removing the tissue paper and revealing a gleaming calfskin brief case.

". . . in the form of this first-class article from Shad Whitmore's shop."

"Boy," he said, addressing me, "take this prize and keep it well. Consider it a badge of office. Prize it. Keep developing as you are and some day it will be filled with important papers that will help shape the destiny of your people."

I was so moved that I could hardly express my thanks. A rope of bloody saliva forming a shape like an undiscovered continent drooled upon the leather and I wiped it quickly away. I felt an importance that I have never dreamed.

"Open it and see what's inside," I was told.

My fingers a-tremble, I complied, smelling the fresh leather and finding an official-looking document inside. It was a scholarship to the state college for Negroes. My eyes filled with tears and I ran awkwardly off the floor.

I was overjoyed; I did not even mind when I discovered that the gold pieces I had scrambled for were brass pocket tokens advertising a certain make of automobile.

When I reached home everyone was excited. Next day the neighbours came to congratulate me. I even felt safe from grandfather, whose deathbed curse usually spoiled my triumphs. I stood beneath his photograph with my brief case in hand and smiled triumphantly into his stolid black peasant's face. It was a face that fascinated me. The eyes seemed to follow everywhere I went.

That night I dreamed I was at a circus with him and that he refused to laugh at the clowns no matter what they did. Then later he told me to open my brief case and read what was inside and I did, finding an official envelope stamped with the state seal; and inside the envelope I found another and another, endlessly, and I thought I would fall of weariness. "Them's years," he said. "Now open that one." And I did and in it I found an engraved document containing a short message in letters of gold. "Read it," my grandfather said. "Out loud."

"To Whom It may Concern," I intoned. "Keep This Nigger Boy Running."

I awoke with the old man's laughter ringing in my ears.

(It was a dream I was to remember and dream again for many years after. But at that time I had no insight into its meaning. First I had to attend college.)

Follow-up

1   Why do you think the leading white citizens of the town want
    to hear the speech, in which the boy shows "that humility was
    the secret, indeed, the very essence of progress"?
2   Describe in detail the ways in which the eminent citizens of the
    town behave during the episode described in the extract. In what
    ways do they use the black boys and why do they act in this
    way?
3   What mistake does the boy make in his speech? Why does his
    mistake so displease the white men?
4   What do you think is the significance of the part the boy's
    grandfather plays in this episode?

The Death of Tod Clifton

from *Invisible Man* by Ralph Ellison, 1947

This episode comes towards the end of the novel, Invisible Man.
*The narrator, having been through a variety of experiences, has
joined the Communist Party and is attempting to express his identity
and assert himself through politics. Because he has a gift for public
speaking he quickly becomes an important figure in the Brotherhood.
One of those closest to him in the Party is Tod Clifton. But Clifton
becomes disillusioned with the Party and to express his despair
becomes a street vendor selling sambo puppets. The narrator happens
to see him one day at his new trade. He watches Clifton being moved
on by the police for illegal street selling. The policeman harasses
Clifton who eventually retaliates and knocks the policeman down.
The policeman gets up and shoots Clifton dead.
After that the narrator gives a speech at his friend's funeral. The
party expects him to give a political speech and to rally the people
into a defiant and revolutionary mood. But when the time comes, his
despair takes over from political commitment; this marks the
beginning of his break from communism.*

Someone nudged me and I started. It was time for final words. But
I had no words and I'd never been to a Brotherhood funeral and

had no idea of a ritual. But they were waiting. I stood there alone; there was no microphone to support me, only the coffin before me upon the backs of its wobbly carpenter's horses.

I looked down into their sun-swept faces, digging for the words, and feeling a futility about it all and an anger. For this they gathered by thousands. What were they waiting to hear? Why had they come? For what reason that was different from that which had made the red-cheeked boy thrill at Clifton's falling to the earth? What did they want and what could they do? Why hadn't they come when they could have stopped it all?

"What are you waiting for me to tell you?" I shouted suddenly, my voice strangely crisp on the windless air. "What good will it do? What if I say that this isn't a funeral, that it's a holiday celebration, that if you stick around the band will end up playing 'Dammit-the-Hell the Fun's All Over'? Or do you expect to see some magic, the dead rise up and walk again? Go home, he's as dead as he'll ever die. That's the end in the beginning and there's no encore. There'll be no miracles and there's no one here to preach a sermon. Go home, forget him. He's inside this box, newly dead. Go home and don't think about him. He's dead and you've got all you can do to think about you." I paused. They were whispering and looking upward.

"I've told you to go home," I shouted, "but you keep standing there. Don't you know it's hot out here in the sun? So what if you wait for what little I can tell you? Can I say in twenty minutes what was building twenty-one years and ended in twenty seconds? What are you waiting for, when all I can tell you is his name? And when I tell you, what will you know that you didn't know already, except perhaps, his name?"

They were listening intently, and as though looking not at me, but at the pattern of my voice upon the air.

"All right, you do the listening in the sun and I'll try to tell you in the sun. Then you go home and forget it. Forget it. His name was Clifton and they shot him down. His name was Clifton and he was tall and some folks thought him handsome. And though he didn't believe it, I think he was. His name was Clifton and his face was black and his hair was thick with tight-rolled curls – or call them naps or kinks. He's dead, uninterested, and, except to a few young girls, it doesn't matter . . . Have you got it? Can you see him? Think of your brother or your cousin John. His lips were thick with an upward curve at the corners. He often smiled. He had good eyes and a pair of fast hands, and he had a heart. He thought about things and he felt deeply. I won't call him noble because what's such a word to do with one of us? His name was Clifton, Tod Clifton, and, like any man, he was born of woman to live awhile and fall and die. So that's his tale to the minute. His name was Clifton and for a while he lived among us and aroused a few hopes in the young manhood of man, and we who knew him loved him and he died. So why are you waiting? You've heard it all. Why wait for more, when all I can do is repeat it?"

They stood; they listened. They gave no sign.

"Very well, so I'll tell you. His name was Clifton and he was young and he was a leader and when he fell there was a hole in the heel of his sock and when he stretched forward he seemed not as tall as he stood. So he died; and we who loved him are gathered here to mourn him. It's as simple as that and as short as that. His name was Clifton and he was black and they shot him. Isn't that enough to tell? Isn't it all you need to know? Isn't that enough to appease your thirst for drama and send you home to sleep it off? Go take a drink and forget it. Or read it in the *Daily News*. His name was Clifton and they shot him, and I was there to see him fall. So I know it as I know it.

"Here are the facts. He was standing and he fell. He fell and he kneeled. He kneeled and he bled. He bled and he died. He fell in a heap like any man and his blood spilled out like any blood; *red* as any blood, wet as any blood and reflecting the sky and the buildings and birds and trees, or your face if you'd looked into its dulling mirror – and it dried in the sun as blood dries. That's all. They spilled his blood and he bled. They cut him down and he died; the blood flowed on the walk in a pool, gleamed a while, and, after a while, became dull then dusty, then dried. That's the story and that's how it ended. It's an old story and there's been too much blood to excite you. Besides, it's only important when it fills the veins of a living man. Aren't you tired of such stories? Aren't you sick of the blood? Then why listen, why don't you go? It's hot out here. There's the odour of embalming fluid. The beer is cold in the taverns, the saxophones will be mellow at the Savoy; plenty good-laughing-lies will be told in the barber shops and beauty parlours; and there'll be sermons in two hundred churches in the cool of the evening, and plenty of laughs at the movies. Go listen to 'Amos and Andy' and forget it. Here you have only the same old story. There's not even a young wife up here in red to mourn him. There's nothing here to pity, no one to break down and shout. Nothing to give you that good old frightened feeling. The story's too short and too simple. His name was Clifton, Tod Clifton, he was unarmed and his death was as senseless as his life was futile. He had struggled for Brotherhood on a hundred street corners and he thought it would make him more human, but he died like any dog in a road.

"All right, all right," I called out, feeling desperate. It wasn't the way I wanted it to go, it wasn't political. Brother Jack probably wouldn't approve of it at all, but I had to keep going as I could go.

"Listen to me standing up on this so-called mountain!" I shouted. "Let me tell it as it truly was! His name was Tod Clifton and he was full of illusions. He thought he was a man when he was only Tod Clifton. He was shot for a simple mistake of judgement and he bled and his blood dried and shortly the crowd trampled out the stains. It was a normal mistake of which many are guilty: He thought he was a man and that men were not meant to be pushed around. But it was hot down-town and he forgot his history, he forgot the time and the place. He lost his hold on reality. There was a cop and a waiting audience but he was Tod Clifton and cops are everywhere. The cop? What about him? He was a cop. A good citizen. But this cop had an itching finger and an eager ear for a word that rhymed with 'trigger', and when Clifton fell he had found it. The Police Special spoke its lines and the rhyme was completed. Just look around you. Look at what he made, look inside you and feel his awful power. It was perfectly natural. The blood ran like blood in a comic-book killing, on a comic-book street in a comic-book town on a comic-book day in a comic-book world.

"Tod Clifton's one with the ages. But what's that to do with you in this heat under this veiled sun? Now he's part of history, and he has received his true freedom. Didn't they scribble his name on a standardized pad? His Race: coloured! Religion: unknown, probably born Baptist. Place of birth: U.S. Some southern town. Next of kin: unknown. Address: unknown. Occupation: unemployed. Cause of death (be specific): resisting reality in the form of a .38 calibre revolver in the hands of the arresting officer, on Forty-second between the library and the subway in the heat of the afternoon, of gunshot wounds received from three bullets, fired at three paces, one bullet entering the right ventricle of the heart, and lodging there, the other severing the spinal ganglia travelling downward to lodge in the pelvis, the other breaking through the back and travelling God knows where.

"Such was the short bitter life of Brother Tod Clifton. Now he's in this box with the bolts tightened down. He's in the box and we're in there with him, and when I've told you this you can go. It's dark in this box and it's crowded. It has a cracked ceiling and a clogged-up toilet in the hall. It has rats and roaches, and it's far, far too expensive a dwelling. The air is bad and it'll be cold this winter. Tod Clifton is crowded and he needs the room. 'Tell them to get out of the box', that's what he would say if you could hear him. 'Tell them to get out of the box and go teach the cops to forget that rhyme. Tell them to teach them that when they call you *nigger* to make a rhyme with *trigger* it makes the gun backfire.'

"So there you have it. In a few hours Tod Clifton will be cold bones in the ground. And don't be fooled, for these bones shall not rise again. You and I will still be in the box. I don't know if Tod Clifton had a soul. I only know the ache that I feel in my heart, my sense of loss. I don't know if *you* have a soul. I only know you are men of flesh and blood; and that blood will spill and flesh grow cold. I do not know if all cops are poets, but I know that all cops carry guns with triggers. And I know too how we are labelled. So in the name of Brother Clifton beware of the triggers; go home, keep cool, stay safe away from the sun. Forget him. When he was alive he was our hope, but why worry over a hope that's dead? So there's only one thing left to tell and I've already told it. His name was Tod Clifton, he believed in Brotherhood, he aroused our hopes and he died."

I couldn't go on. Below, they were waiting, hands and handkerchiefs shading their eyes. A preacher stepped up and read something out of his Bible, and I stood looking at the crowd with a sense of failure. I had let it get away from me, had been unable to bring in the political issues. And they stood there sun-beaten and sweat-bathed, listening to me repeat what was known. Now the preacher had finished, and someone signalled the bandmaster and there was solemn music as the pall-bearers carried the coffin down the spiralling stairs. The crowd stood still as we walked slowly through. I could feel the bigness of it and the unknownness of it and a pent-up tension – whether of tears or anger, I couldn't tell. But as we walked through and down the hill to the hearse, I could feel it. The crowd sweated and throbbed, and though it was silent, there were many things directed towards me through its eyes. At the kerb were the hearse and a few cars, and in a few minutes they were loaded and the crowd was still standing, looking on as we carried Tod Clifton away. And as I took one last look I saw not a crowd but the set faces of individual men and women.

We drove away and when the cars stopped moving there was a

grave and we placed him in it. The gravediggers sweated heavily and knew their business and their brogue was Irish. They filled the grave quickly and we left. Tod Clifton was underground.

I returned through the streets as tired as though I'd dug the grave myself alone. I felt confused and listless moving through the crowds that seemed to boil along in a kind of mist, as though the thin humid clouds had thickened and settled directly above our heads. I wanted to go somewhere, to some cool place to rest without thinking, but there was still too much to be done; plans had to be made; the crowd's emotion had to be organized. I crept along, walking a southern walk in southern weather, closing my eyes from time to time against the dazzling reds, yellows and greens of cheap sport shirts and summer dresses. The crowd boiled, sweated, heaved; women with shopping bags, men with highly polished shoes. Even down South they'd always shined their shoes. "Shined shoes, shoed shines", it rang in my head. On Eighth Avenue, the market carts were parked hub to hub along the kerb, improvised canopies shading the withering fruits and vegetables. I could smell the stench of decaying cabbage. A watermelon huckster stood in the shade beside his truck, holding up a long slice of orange-meated melon, crying his wares with hoarse appeals to nostalgia, memories of childhood, green shade and summer coolness. Oranges, coconuts and alligator pears lay in neat piles on little tables. I passed, winding my way through the slowly moving crowd. Stale and wilted flowers, rejected downtown, blazed feverishly on a cart, like glamorous rags festering beneath a futile spray from a punctured fruit juice can. The crowd were boiling figures seen through steaming glass from inside a washing machine; and in the streets the mounted police detail stood looking on, their eyes non-committal beneath the short polished visors of their caps, their bodies slanting forward, reins slackly alert, men and horses of flesh imitating men and horses of stone. Tod Clifton's *Tod*, I thought. The hucksters cried above the traffic sounds and I seemed to hear them from a distance, unsure of what they said. In a side street children with warped tricycles were parading along the walk carrying one of the signs,

BROTHER TOD CLIFTON, OUR HOPE SHOT DOWN.

And through the haze I again felt the tension. There was no denying it; it was there and something had to be done before it simmered away in the heat.

Follow-up

1 Try and describe what you think the hero's feelings are about what has happened to Tod Clifton.
2 The hero is an excellent public speaker. What techniques does he use to get through to the emotions of the crowd?
3 What do you think he means when he says "His name was Tod Clifton and he was full of illusions. He thought he was a man when he was only Tod Clifton"?

Richard and Elizabeth

from *Go Tell it on the Mountain* by James Baldwin, 1954

This novel deals with a moment of crisis in the life of an adolescent boy, John, living in America during the 1930s. He has to try to decide between the ways of the Lord that his parents want him to follow and what they see as the ways of sin. The novel flashes back from this present to the lives of those adults close to John who are influencing him in this decision. In this extract we learn about the brief and tragic relationship of his mother, Elizabeth, and his real father, Richard. His mother makes a bid for her happiness by moving to New York to be with the man she loves. The difficult but passionate relationship that consumes her youth is tragically destroyed by the pressures of a prejudiced society. Her spirit dies when her love is destroyed and she retreats into the joyless religious world of the man she later marries.

The extract begins at the moment when Elizabeth has followed Richard from the South to New York, much against the wishes of the aunt who has been looking after her.

Her pretext for coming to New York was to take advantage of the greater opportunities the North offered coloured people; to study in a Northern school, and to find a better job than any she was likely to be offered in the South. Her aunt, who listened to this with no diminution of her habitual scorn, was yet unable to deny that from generation to generation things, as she grudgingly put it, were bound to change – and neither could she quite take the position of seeming to stand in Elizabeth's way. In the winter of 1920, as the year began, Elizabeth found herself in an ugly back room in Harlem in the home of her aunt's relative, a woman whose respectability was immediately evident from the incense she burned in her rooms and the spiritualist séances she held every Saturday night.

The house was still standing, not very far away; often she was forced to pass it. Without looking up, she was able to see the windows of the apartment in which she had lived, and the woman's sign, which was in the window still: MADAME WILLIAMS, SPIRITUALIST.

She found a job as chambermaid in the same hotel in which Richard worked as elevator boy. Richard said that they would marry as soon as he had saved some money. But since he was going to school at night and made very little money, their marriage, which she had thought of as taking place almost as soon as she arrived, was planned for a future that grew ever more remote. And this presented her with a problem that she had refused, at home in Maryland, to think about, but from which, now, she could not escape: the problem of their life together. Reality, so to speak, burst in for the first time on her great dreaming, and she found occasion to wonder, ruefully, what had made her imagine that, once with Richard, she would have been able to withstand him. She had kept, precariously enough, what her aunt referred to as her pearl without price while she had been with Richard down home. This, which she had taken as witness to her own feminine moral strength, had been due to nothing more, it now developed, than her great fear of her aunt, and the lack, in that small town, of opportunity. Here, in this great city where no one cared, where people might live in the same building for years and never speak to one another, she found herself, when Richard took her in his arms, on the edge of a steep place: and down she rushed, on the descent uncaring, into the dreadful sea.

So it began. Had it been waiting for her since the day she had been taken from her father's arms? The world in which she now found herself was not unlike the world from which she had, so long ago, been rescued. Here were the women who had been the cause of her aunt's most passionate condemnation of her father – hard-drinking, hard-talking, with whisky- and cigarette-breath, and moving with the mystic authority of women who knew what sweet violence might be acted out under the moon and stars, or beneath the tigerish lights of the city, in the raucous hay or the singing bed. And was she, Elizabeth, so sweetly fallen, so tightly chained, one of these women now? And here were the men who had come day and night to visit her father's "stable" – with their sweet talk and their music, and their violence and their sex – black, brown, and beige, who looked on her with lewd, and lustful, and laughing eyes. And these were Richard's friends. Not one of them ever went to church – one might scarcely have imagined that they knew that churches existed – they all, hourly, daily, in their speech, in their lives, and in their hearts, cursed God. They all seemed to be saying, as Richard, when she once timidly mentioned the love of Jesus, said: "You can tell that puking bastard to kiss my big black ass."

She, for very terror on hearing this, had wept; yet she could not deny that for such an abundance of bitterness there was a positive fountain of grief. There was not, after all, a great difference between the world of the North and that of the South which she had fled; there was only this difference: the North promised more. And this similarity: what it promised it did not give, and what it gave, at length and grudgingly with one hand, it took back with the other. Now she understood in this nervous, hollow, ringing city, that nervousness of Richard's which had so attracted her – a tension so total, and so without the hope, or possibility of release, or resolution, that she felt it in his muscles, and heard it in his breathing, even as on her breast he fell asleep.

And this was perhaps why she had never thought to leave him, frightened though she was during all that time, and in a world in which, had it not been for Richard, she could have found no place to put her feet. She did not leave him, because she was afraid of what might happen to him without her. She did not resist him, because he needed her. And she did not press about marriage because, upset as he was about everything, she was afraid of having him upset about her, too. She thought of herself as his strength; in a world of shadows, the indisputable reality to which he could always repair. And, again, for all that had come, she could not regret this. She had tried, but she had never been and was not now, even tonight, truly sorry. Where, then, was her repentance? And how could God hear her cry?

They had been very happy together, in the beginning; and until the very end he had been very good to her, had not ceased to love her, and tried always to make her know it. No more than she had been able to accuse her father had she ever been able to accuse him. His weakness, she understood, and his terror, and even his bloody end. What life had made him bear, her lover, this wild, unhappy boy, many another stronger and more virtuous man might not have borne so well.

Saturday was their best day, for they only worked until one o'clock. They had all the afternoon to be together, and nearly all of the night, since Madame Williams had her séances on Saturday night and preferred that Elizabeth, before whose silent scepticism departed spirits might find themselves reluctant to speak, should not be in the house. They met at the service entrance. Richard was always there before her looking, oddly, much younger and less anonymous without the ugly, tight-fitting, black uniform that he had to wear when working. He would be talking, or laughing with some of the other boys, or shooting craps, and when he heard her step down the long, stone hall he would look up, laughing; and wickedly nudging one of the other boys, he would half shout, half sing: "Hey-y! Look-a-there, ain't she pretty?"

She never failed at this — which was why he never failed to do it — to blush, half-smiling, half-frowning, and nervously to touch the collar of her dress.

"*Sweet* Georgia Brown!" somebody might say.

"*Miss* Brown to you," said Richard, then, and took her arm.

"Yeah, that's right," somebody else would say, "you *better* hold on to little Miss Bright-eyes, don't somebody sure going to take her away from you."

"Yeah," said another voice, "and it might be me."

"*Oh*, no," said Richard, moving with her toward the street, "ain't nobody going to take *my* little Little-bit away from *me*."

Little-bit: it had been his name for her. And sometimes he called her Sandwich Mouth, or Funnyface, or Frog-eyes. She would not, of course, have endured these names from anyone else nor, had she not found herself, with joy and helplessness (and a sleeping panic), living it out, would she ever have suffered herself so publicly to become a man's property — "concubine", her aunt would have said, and at night, alone, she rolled the word, tart like lemon rind, on her tongue.

She was descending with Richard to the sea. She would have to climb back up alone, but she did not know this then. Leaving the boys in the hall, they gained the midtown New York streets.

"And what we going to do today, Little-bit?" With that smile of his, and those depthless eyes, beneath the towers of the white city, with people, white, hurrying all around them.

"I don't know, honey. What you want to do?"

"Well, maybe, we go to a *mu*seum."

The first time he suggested this, she demanded, in panic, if they would be allowed to enter.

"Sure, they let niggers in," Richard said. "Ain't we got to be educated, too – to live with the motherf——s?"

He never "watched" his language with her, which at first she took as evidence of his contempt because she had fallen so easily, and which later she took as evidence of his love.

And when he took her to the Museum of Natural History, or the Metropolitan Museum of Art, where they were almost certain to be the only black people, and he guided her through the halls, which never ceased in her imagination to be as cold as tombstones, it was then she saw another life in him. It never ceased to frighten her, this passion he brought to something she could not understand.

For she never grasped – not at any rate with her mind – what, with such incandescence, he tried to tell her on these Saturday afternoons. She could not find, between herself and the African statuette, or totem pole, on which he gazed with such melancholy wonder, any point of contact. She was only glad that she did not look that way. She preferred to look, in the other museum, at the paintings; but still she did not understand anything he said about them. She did not know why he so adored things that were so long dead; what sustenance they gave him, what secrets he hoped to wrest from them. But she understood, at least, that they *did* give him a kind of bitter nourishment, and that the secrets they held for him were a matter of his life and death. It frightened her because she felt that he was reaching for the moon and that he would, therefore, be dashed down against the rocks; but she did not say any of this. She only listened, and in her heart she prayed for him.

But on other Saturdays they went to see a movie; they went to see a play; they visited his friends; they walked through Central Park. She liked the park because, however spuriously, it recreated something of the landscape she had known. How many afternoons had they walked there! She had always, since, avoided it. They bought peanuts and for hours fed the animals at the zoo; they bought soda pop and drank it on the grass; they walked along the reservoir and Richard explained how a city like New York found water to drink. Mixed with her fear for him was a total admiration: that he had learned so young, so much. People stared at them but she did not mind; he noticed, but he did not seem to notice. But sometimes he would ask, in the middle of a sentence – concerned, possibly, with ancient Rome:

"Little-bit – d'you love me?"

And she wondered how he could doubt it. She thought how infirm she must be not to have been able to make him know it; and she raised her eyes to his, and she said the only thing she could say:

"I wish to God I may die if I don't love you. There ain't no sky above us if I don't love you."

Then he would look ironically up at the sky, and take her arm with a firmer pressure, and they would walk on.

Once, she asked him:

"Richard, did you go to school much when you was little?"

And he looked at her a long moment. Then:

"Baby, I done told you, my mama died when I was born. And my daddy, he weren't nowhere to be found. Ain't nobody never took care of me. I just moved from one place to another. When one set of folks got tired of me they sent me down the line. I didn't hardly go to school at all."

"Then how come you got to be so smart? How come you got to know so much?"

And he smiled, pleased, but he said: "Little-bit, I don't know so much." Then he said, with a change in his face and voice which she had grown to know: "I just decided me one day that I was going to get to know everything them white bastards knew, and I was going to get to know it better than them, so could no white son-of-a-bitch *nowhere* never talk *me* down, and never make me feel like *I* was dirt, when I could read him the alphabet, back, front, and sideways. Shit – he weren't going to beat my ass, then. And if he tried to kill me, I'd take him with me, I swear to my mother I would." Then he looked at her again, and smiled and kissed her, and he said: "That's how I got to know so much, baby."

She asked: "And what you going to do, Richard? What you want to be?"

And his face clouded. "I don't know. I got to find out. Looks like I can't get my mind straight nohow."

She did not know *why* he couldn't – or she could only dimly face it – but she knew he spoke the truth.

She had made her great mistake with Richard in not telling him that she was going to have a child. Perhaps, she thought now, if she had told him everything might have been very different, and he would be living yet. But the circumstances under which she had discovered herself to be pregnant had been such to make her decide, for his sake, to hold her peace awhile. Frightened as she was, she dared not add to the panic that overtook him on the last summer of his life.

And yet perhaps it was, after all, this – this failure to demand of his strength what it might then, most miraculously, have been found able to bear; by which – indeed, how could she know? – his strength might have been strengthened, for which she prayed tonight to be forgiven. Perhaps she had lost her love because she had not, in the end, believed in it enough.

She lived quite a long way from Richard – four subway stops; and when it was time for her to go home, he always took the subway uptown with her and walked her to her door. On a Saturday when they had forgotten the time and stayed together later than usual, he left her at her door at two o'clock in the morning. They said good night hurriedly, for she was afraid of trouble when she got upstairs – though, in fact, Madame Williams seemed astonishingly indifferent to the hours Elizabeth kept – and he wanted to hurry back home and go to bed. Yet, as he hurried off down the dark, murmuring street, she had a sudden impulse to call him back, to ask him to take her with him and never let her go again. She hurried up the steps, smiling a little at this fancy: it was because he looked so young and defenceless as he walked away, and yet so jaunty and strong.

He was to come the next evening at suppertime, to make at last, at Elizabeth's urging, the acquaintance of Madame Williams. But he did not come. She drove Madame Williams wild with her sudden sensitivity to footsteps on the stairs. Having told Madame Williams that a gentleman was coming to visit her, she did not dare, of course, to leave the house and go out looking for him, thus giving Madame Williams the impression that she dragged men in off the streets. At ten o'clock, having eaten no supper, a detail unnoticed by her hostess, she went to bed, her head aching and her heart sick with fear; fear over what had happened to Richard, who had never kept her waiting before; and fear involving all that was beginning to happen in her body.

And on Monday morning he was not at work. She left during the lunch hour to go to his room. He was not there. His landlady said that he had not been there all weekend. While Elizabeth stood trembling and indecisive in the hall, two white policemen entered.

She knew the moment she saw them, and before they mentioned his name, that something terrible had happened to Richard. Her heart, as on that bright summer day when he had first spoken to her, gave a terrible bound and then was still, with an awful, wounded stillness. She put out one hand to touch the wall in order to keep standing.

"This here young lady was just looking for him," she heard the landlady say.

They all looked at her.

"You his girl?" one of the policemen asked.

She looked up at his sweating face, on which a lascivious smile had immediately appeared, and straightened, trying to control her trembling.

"Yes," she said. "Where is he?"

"He's in jail, honey," the other policeman said.

"What for?"

"For robbing a white man's store, black girl. That's what for."

She found, and thanked Heaven for it, that a cold, stony rage had entered her. She would, otherwise, certainly have fallen down, or began to weep. She looked at the smiling policeman.

"Richard ain't robbed no store," she said. "Tell me where he is."

"And *I* tell you," he said, not smiling, "that your boyfriend robbed a store and he's in jail for it. He's going to stay there, too – now, what you got to say to that?"

"And he probably did it for you, too," the other policeman said. "You look like a girl a man could rob a store for."

She said nothing; she was thinking how to get to see him, how to get him out.

One of them, the smiler, turned now to the landlady and said: "Let's have the key to his room. How long's he been living here?"

"About a year," the landlady said. She looked unhappily at Elizabeth. "He seemed like a real nice boy."

"Ah, yes," he said, mounting the steps, "they all seem like real nice boys when they pay their rent."

"You going to take me to see him?" she asked of the remaining policeman. She found herself fascinated by the gun in his holster, the club at his side. She wanted to take that pistol and empty it into his round, red face; to take that club and strike with all her strength against the base of his skull where his cap ended, until the ugly, silky, white man's hair was matted with blood and brains.

"Sure, girl," he said, "you're coming right along with us. The man at the station house wants to ask you some questions."

The smiling policeman came down again. "Ain't nothing up there," he said. "Let's go."

She moved between them, out into the sun. She knew that there was nothing to be gained by talking to them any more. She was entirely in their power; she would have to think faster than they could think; she would have to contain her fear and her hatred, and find out what could be done. Not for anything short of Richard's life, and not, possibly, even for that, would she have wept before them, or asked of them a kindness.

A small crowd, children and curious passers-by, followed them as they walked the long, dusty, sunlit street. She hoped only that they would not pass anyone she knew; she kept her head high, looking straight ahead, and felt the skin settle over her bones as though she were wearing a mask.

And at the station she somehow got past their brutal laughter. (*What was he doing with you, girl, until two o'clock in the morning? – Next time you feel like that, girl, you come by here and talk to* me.) She felt that she was about to burst, or vomit, or die. Though the sweat stood out cruelly, like needles on her brow, and she felt herself, from every side, being covered with a stink and filth, she found out, in their own good time, what she wanted to know: He was being held in a prison downtown called the Tombs (the name made her heart turn over), and she could see him tomorrow. The state, or the prison, or someone, had already assigned him a lawyer; he would be brought to trial next week.

But the next day, when she saw him, she wept. He had been beaten, he whispered to her, and he could hardly walk. His body, she later discovered, bore almost no bruises, but was full of strange, painful swellings, and there was a welt above one eye.

He had not, of course, robbed the store but, when he left her that Saturday night, had gone down into the subway station to wait for his train. It was late, and trains were slow; he was all alone on the platform, only half awake, thinking, he said, of her.

Then, from the far end of the platform, he heard a sound of running; and, looking up, he saw two coloured boys come running down the steps. Their clothes were torn, and they were frightened; they came up the platform and stood near him, breathing hard. He was about to ask them what the trouble was when, running across the tracks toward them, and followed by a white man, he saw another coloured boy; and at the same instant another white man came running down the subway steps.

Then he came full awake, in panic; he knew that whatever the trouble was, it was now his trouble also; for these white men would make no distinction between him and the three boys they were after: They were all coloured, they were about the same age, and here they stood together on the subway platform. And they were all, with no questions asked, herded upstairs, and into the wagon and to the station house.

At the station Richard gave his name and address and age and occupation. Then for the first time he stated that he was not involved, and asked one of the other boys to corroborate his testimony. This they rather despairingly did. They might, Elizabeth felt, have done it sooner, but they probably also felt that it would be useless to speak. And they were not believed; the owner of the store was being brought there to make the identification. And Richard tried to relax: the man *could* not say that he had been there if he had never seen him before.

But when the owner came, a short man with a bloody shirt – for they had knifed him – in the company of yet another policeman, he looked at the four boys before him and said: "Yeah, that's them, all right."

Then Richard shouted: "But *I* wasn't there! Look at me, goddammit – I wasn't *there!*"

"You black bastards," the man said, looking at him, "you're all the same."

Then there was silence in the station, the eyes of the white men all watching. And Richard said, but quietly, knowing that he was lost: "But all the same, mister, I wasn't there." And he looked at the white man's bloody shirt and thought, he told Elizabeth, at the bottom of his heart: "I wish to God they'd killed you."

Then the questioning began. The three boys signed a confession at once, but Richard would not sign. He said at last that he would die before he signed a confession to something he hadn't done. "Well then," said one of them, hitting him suddenly across the head, "maybe you *will* die, you black son-of-a-bitch." And the beating began. He would not, then, talk to her about it; she found that, before the dread and the hatred that filled her mind, her imagination faltered and held its peace.

"What we going to do?" she asked at last.

He smiled a vicious smile – she had never seen such a smile on his face before. "Maybe you ought to pray to that Jesus of yours and get Him to come down and tell these white men something." He looked at her a long, dying moment. "Because I don't know nothing else to do," he said.

She suggested: "Richard, what about another lawyer?"

And he smiled again. "I declare," he said, "Little-bit's been holding out on me. She got a fortune tied up in a sock, and she ain't never told me nothing about it."

She had been trying to save money for a whole year, but she had only thirty dollars. She sat before him, going over in her mind all the things she might do to raise money, even to going on the streets. Then, for very helplessness, she began to shake with sobbing. At this, his face became Richard's face again. He said in a shaking voice: "Now, look here, Little-bit, don't you be like that. We going to work this out all right." But she could not stop sobbing. "Elizabeth," he whispered, "Elizabeth, Elizabeth." Then the man came and said that it was time for her to go. And she rose. She had brought two packs of cigarettes for him, and they were still in her bag. Wholly ignorant of prison regulations, she did not dare to give them to him under the man's eyes. And, somehow, her failure to remember to give him the cigarettes, when she knew how much he smoked, made her weep the harder. She tried – and failed – to smile at him, and she was slowly led to the door. The sun nearly blinded her, and she heard him whisper behind her: "So long, baby. Be good."

In the streets she did not know what to do. She stood awhile before the dreadful gates, and then she walked and walked until she came to a coffee shop where taxi drivers and the people who worked in nearby offices hurried in and out all day. Usually she was afraid to go into downtown establishments, where only white people were, but today she did not care. She felt that if anyone said anything to her she would turn and curse him like the lowest bitch on the streets. If anyone touched her, she would do her best to send his soul to Hell.

But no one touched her; no one spoke. She drank her coffee, sitting in the strong sun that fell through the window. Now it came to her how alone, how frightened she was; she had never been so frightened in her life before. She knew that she was pregnant – knew it, as the old folks said, in her bones; and if Richard should be sent away what, under Heaven, could she do? Two years, three years – she had no idea how long he might be sent away for – what would she do? And how could she keep her aunt from knowing? And if her aunt should find out, then her father would know, too. The tears welled up, and she drank her cold, tasteless coffee. And what would they do with Richard? And if they sent him away, what would he be like, then, when he returned? She looked out into the quiet, sunny streets, and for the first time in her life, she hated it all – the white city, the white world. She could not, that day, think of one decent white person in the whole world. She sat there, and she hoped that one day God, with tortures inconceivable, would grind them utterly into humility, and make them know that black boys and black girls, whom they treated with such condescension, such disdain, and such good humour, had hearts like human beings, too, more human hearts than theirs.

But Richard was not sent away. Against the testimony of the three robbers, and her own testimony and, under oath, the storekeeper's indecision, there was no evidence on which to convict him. The courtroom seemed to feel, with some complacency and some disappointment, that it was his great good luck to be let off so easily. They went immediately to his room. And there – she was never all her life long to forget it – he threw himself, face downward, on his bed and wept.

She had only seen one other man weep before – her father – and it had not been like this. She touched him, but he did not stop. Her own tears fell on his dirty, uncombed hair. She tried to hold him, but for a long while he would not be held. His body was like iron; she could find no softness in it. She sat curled like a frightened child on the edge of the bed, her hand on his back, waiting for the storm to pass over. It was then that she decided not to tell him yet about the child.

By and by he called her name. And then he turned, and she held him against her breast, while he sighed and shook. He fell asleep at last, clinging to her as though he were going down into the water for the last time.

And it was the last time. That night he cut his wrists with his razor and he was found in the morning by his landlady, his eyes staring upward with no light, dead among the scarlet sheets.

Follow-up

1 Elizabeth discovers in Richard "a tension so total, and so without the hope, or possibility of release, or resolution, that she felt it in his muscles, and heard it in his breathing, even as on her breast he fell asleep". Describe Richard's character and show how this tension dictates his attitudes and behaviour.
2 What is offensive in the behaviour of the policeman when they come to take Elizabeth to the police station?
3 Why doesn't Elizabeth tell Richard she is pregnant and why, afterwards, does she regret this?
4 "You black bastards", the man said, looking at him, "you're all the same." Show how this attitude leads to Richard's arrest and then to his suicide.

Escape Routes

Before the civil rights movement which gathered momentum in
America in the 1960s there seemed few routes which black people
could take to escape the dead-end of racist oppression. Traditional
escape routes were sport, entertainment, and the church. Black
boxers, athletes, singers, and musicians have figured prominently in
twentieth-century America. Music and athletic skill were areas of
success and achievement which white Americans allowed to blacks.
In effect, the system allowed the blacks to entertain the whites.
Muhammad Ali, the most famous black sportsman of all time,
realized very early in his career the role he was expected to play and
he refused to accept it.

James Baldwin, highly intelligent and talented, but not an athlete
or musician, initially saw his escape route through the church. The
church could provide status and power for the black man within his
own community, respectability in the eyes of the whites and God's
love and forgiveness. It therefore held powerful attractions.

Olympic Gold

from *The Greatest – My Own Story* by Muhammad Ali, 1976

*Muhammad Ali is one of the best-known and best-loved men in the
whole world. People everywhere have admired his supreme skill
and been made happy by his humour and his great enthusiasm for
life. But he has had to struggle to achieve his success and he has not
escaped the problems and frustrations that are brought through
being a black man in America.*

*In the extract that follows he learns that while, on one level, the
people of Louisville can welcome him as an Olympic hero, on
another level he is still a black "boy" who cannot be served at white
restaurants. What follows from his attempts to get service in a white
restaurant helps to shape his whole future attitude to his blackness.*

*The extract begins with Muhammad returning to Louisville, his
home town, as the 1960 Olympic heavyweight gold medallist, ready
to sign a professional contract.*

So what I remember most about the summer of 1960 is not the
hero welcome, the celebrations, the Police Chief, the Mayor, the
Governor, or even the ten Louisville millionaires, but that night
when I stood on the Jefferson County Bridge and threw my
Olympic Gold Medal down to the bottom of the Ohio River.

A few minutes earlier I had fought a man almost to death because
he wanted to take it from me, just as I had been willing to fight to
the death in the ring to win it.

It had taken six years of blood, blows, pain, sweat, struggle, a
thousand rounds in rings and gyms to win that medal, a prize I had
dreamed of holding since I was a child. Now I had thrown it in the
river. And I felt no pain and no regret. Only relief, and a new
strength.

I had turned pro. In my pocket was my agreement with the ten
Louisville millionaires, our "marriage contract" for six years. I felt as
sure as day and night that I would one day be the World
Heavyweight Champion. But my Olympic honeymoon as a White
Hope had ended. It was not a change I wanted to tell the world
about yet. I would be champion. My own kind of champion.

The honeymoon had started when my plane touched down at
Standiford Field. They opened the door and my mother rushed up
to hug me. Then my brother Rudy and Dad. I had been gone for

twenty-one days, the most time I'd been away since the day I was born.

Then came the celebrations: the long police escort all the way downtown; black and white crowds on the streets and sidewalks; WELCOME HOME CASSIUS CLAY signs from my classmates at Central High; the Mayor telling me the Olympic Gold Medal was my key to the city; plans under way for me to have my picture taken with President Eisenhower.

Time magazine saying: "Cassius never lets his Gold Medal out of his sight. He even sleeps with it." They were right. I ate with it, and wouldn't stop sleeping with it even though the sharp edges cut my back when I rolled over. Nothing would ever make me part with it. Not even when the "gold" began to wear off, leaving a dull-looking lead base. I wondered why the richest, most powerful nation in the world could not afford to give their Olympic champions real gold.

One Kentucky newspaper described my medal as "the biggest prize any black boy ever brought back to Louisville". But if a white boy had brought back anything better to this city, where only race horses and whisky were important, I hadn't heard about it.

In later years, when I fought and did exhibitions around the world, in Zurich, Cairo, Tokyo, Stockholm, London, Lima, Dublin, Rio de Janiero, I was given welcomes and celebrations that were much greater, more colourful. But when you've been planted like a tree in one town, and suddenly become recognized and acclaimed by the other trees, it is unlike any other experience you are likely to have. In fact, I'd written a poem about it on the plane, "How Cassius Took Rome", which I sent to the black newspapers and later recited to my classmates, a poem expressing my love for Louisville.

And although I was still hit with some of the same race hostility I'd known all my life, my spirits were so high I felt whoever was against me would change. Even those whose resentment made them go through the acknowledgements half-heartedly or with no heart at all. Those who came only out of curiosity, and looked disgusted when they learned they had to honour a black boy.

I was deeply proud of having represented America on a world stage. To me the Gold Medal was more than a symbol of what I had achieved for myself and my country; there was something I expected the medal to achieve for me. And during those first days of homecoming it seemed to be doing exactly that.

I remember the crowds that followed us down the street where we lived. The porch of our house was decked with American flags, and my father had painted the steps red, white and blue. Photographers yelled, "Hold it! Hold it!" And I posed for a minute, arm-in-arm with my father as he sang "'The Star-Spangled Banner" in his best Russ Columbo style. We stood proud. Everybody cheered.

Through most of that summer the crowds kept coming around the house. Louisville lit up. Congratulations every day from city officials. Even handshakes from the Chief of Police. A slap on the back from the Governor of Kentucky, who reminded me, "Boy, I know you proud of that name 'Cassius Clay'. I know you proud to carry that name."

In the evenings we sifted through offers from professionals to "manage" me. One telegram from Archie Moore: IF YOU DESIRE TO HAVE AN EXCELLENT MANAGER CALL ME COLLECT. From Rocky Marciano: YOU HAVE THE PROMISE. I CAN GIVE YOU THE GUIDANCE. From Cus D'Amato, Floyd Patterson's manager. From Pete Rademacher, former Olympic Champion. We examined every offer until a lawyer came representing ten (later eleven) Louisville millionaires, who put together the contract my father and family approved. It was to run from 1960 to 1966, and it did. The main feature was a $10,000 advance. The Louisville group, to start off, was to get 50 per cent of all my earnings, in and out of the ring. At the time $10,000 seemed to me a huge amount. The only frame of reference I had to "big" sums of money was the worn-down little house we lived in. Sold to us on instalment for $4,500, it was taking my father his lifetime to pay for it. Most of the $10,000 went to repair and pay off the house.

In those first days after my return from Rome, I was proud to boast of my millionaire sponsors. It looked like solid evidence that the pain and struggle I had undergone to win national Golden Gloves titles, state and AAU championships had brought me to a point where I could make money from boxing, not only for myself but for my backers. I felt fortunate having so many people in town who wanted to give me what they called the "right kind of moral and ethical environment" for launching a career. As far back as I could remember, boxing was associated with stories of "gangster control", "fixed fights", and "back-door deals", some of it brought out by Kefauver Committee investigations while I was fighting in the Golden Gloves.

The Sunday after I signed, the Reverend Isaiah Brayden, of the Ship of Zion Baptist Church, preached a sermon about it, and said, "May Cassius Clay be eternally grateful for what those kind Christian millionaires are doing for his black soul." Every newspaper account I read described the event in the holiest light, with ten white angels tending charity in the jungle. Not as the good, hard, common-sense business deal it was.

I kept their names in my pocket, ready to pull them out as proof of my status as a top-sponsored fighter, and I meant to display them as much as my Gold Medal.

I had the list for display one afternoon when I rode my new motorbike down to the Mayor's office to let him show my Olympic Medal to some visiting dignitaries. Along with me was Ronald King, a close friend, a good student, one who I copied off of in class.

The Mayor introduced me. "Cassius is a typical Louisville product," he said. "Our next World Champion."

The visitors applauded.

"Y'all hear what Cassius told that old Russian in Rome?" The Mayor was warming up. "Read 'bout that? This old Russian had the nerve to ask our boy how things were for Negroes in America. G'head, Cassius. Tell 'em. Don't be shy."

I saw what was coming. A remark I'd made in Rome, one I regretted. But the Mayor went on:

"He brushed off that Russian reporter like dirt. Tell 'em, Cash. Why, Cassius stood up tall, 'Look here, Commie. America is the best country in the world, including yours. I'd rather live here in Louisville than in Africa 'cause at least I ain't fightin' off no snakes and alligators and livin' in mud huts.' He sho' told 'em!" He put his arms around me. "He's our own boy, Cassius, our next World Champion. Anything you want in town's yourn. You hear that?"

I heard him, and I heard something else inside me that turned over in shame. Of all the things I had said at the Olympic Village, this remark was most quoted in newspapers and magazines, on TV and radio, and repeated month after month, and the instant I made it I felt I had gotten caught up in some big white net. I had given the answer the white reporters, who were listening, wanted to hear a black athlete say. I knew nothing of Russia and little of Africa, except what I'd seen in Tarzan movies. Yet the effect of my answer had been brought home to me my first day in Louisville. A young Nigerian approached me as I was talking with some friends, and asked if I'd been quoted correctly. When I acknowledged that I had, he said, "I thought we were brothers. You don't understand."

I never met him before or since, but his sadness shook me. And I knew I had been slanted in the wrong direction. Later, when I did travel many times to Africa, I was even more ashamed that I had grown up so brainwashed about the history and life of the people I descended from.

Most of the Africans I met and mingled with were far better educated than me, many spoke five and six languages and all spoke

English better than I did. I saw modern cities, met talented, artistic people and got to know something of the culture and contributions Africa had made in the ancient and modern worlds. I learned how Europe and America had robbed, raped and enslaved its people for centuries, and were still plundering and draining its wealth.

That Nigerian's criticism made me cautious about not allowing myself to be groomed, deliberately or not, to become a "White Hope". Of course I understood they would prefer that the White Hope be white. But, Hopes having come upon hard times in boxing, I could see they would settle for a Black White Hope, as long as he believed what they believed, talked the way they talked and hated the people they hated. Until a real White White Hope come around.

Eight years later, barred from boxing in America and forbidden to travel outside the country, I watched the 1968 Olympic boxing matches in Mexico City. I saw George Foreman parade around the ring waving an American flag after his Olympic victory. Not that George usually went around waving American flags. I've never heard of him waving a flag before or since. But he had been put up to it to offset black athletes like Tommy Smith and Carlos Jones, who dramatized before the world their objections to American injustice with their Black Power salute. There was hardly a black or fair-minded white who did not admire Smith and Jones, or who did admire Foreman. And despite his considerable ability as a fighter, his image as an Uncle Tom stuck with him.

Yet I can understand where George was coming from. I had been there before him. It took me a while to learn that while the slave masters cheer for slavery, they get a freakish thrill making the slave cheer for slavery.

That afternoon I left the Mayor's office resolved that if I could not change my remark before the public, I would change it for myself. Little did I know that the first act in this "correction" would begin before I had finished my bike ride.

It was getting cloudy, and Ronnie and I raced our motorbikes across downtown Louisville. There had been a forecast of high wind and heavy rain, and the first sprinkle came when we passed a newly remodelled restaurant. I slowed down.

"Not there, not there!" Ronnie warned and kept his motor going.

But I stopped and parked near a line of big Harley-Davidson hogs. Their owners, a leather-jacketed gang, were sitting at tables near the window with their girl friends. Nazi insignias on their backs, Confederate flags painted on the front, a style popular with some whites in the East End. One they called "Kentucky Slim" I'd seen at my fights. Slim gave me a nod. Their leader, a big redhead with doubled-up leg chains hanging from his shoulder, sat with his arms round a heavy blonde. 'Frog', as we knew him, never looked up, although I knew he saw me.

I found two empty seats at the counter, and as Ronnie caught up I sat down and picked up a menu. A young waitress quickly came up and placed napkins, silverware and a glass of water in front of us.

"Two hamburgers. Two milk shakes, vanilla", Ronnie said, but as the waitress moved back to the kitchen a big, beefy man with a hungover stomach motioned for her to come where he sat near the cash register.

Whatever his words, they were brief. The waitress disappeared inside the kitchen and, after what seemed a long time, appeared again, talking to one of the kitchen help, an old, thin-faced black woman who just stood at the door, looking down my way and trying to say something.

In those days most of the restaurants, hotels and movies in Louisville, as in all the South, were either closed to blacks or had segregated sections.

The white girl finally came back and whispered as though she had something confidential to tell me. "We can't serve you here."

Ronnie muttered under his breath, and I nudged him to be quiet. It felt good to be so calm and prepared for what I thought was coming. My Gold Medal would be the solution to the whole thing.

This was not the first time Ronnie and I had entered a "white only" place, just the first time as "home-grown" Negroes. Once, for Halloween, we had a seamstress make us a couple of African turbans and flowing gowns. We used them for months to masquerade downtown. We would speak "foreign" English and talk to each other in a fast homemade language to get ourselves admitted to "white only" places as foreigners. One time at a movie house a suspicious doorman stopped us, but the white manager called back to him. "It's all right. They ain't Negroes."

Now I felt I had grown. Now there was no need to masquerade as a foreigner. I had whipped all the foreigners to bring the Gold Medal to America. I would use any native language.

"Miss," I began politely, believing she was acting out of ignorance. "I'm Cassius Clay. The Olympic Champion."

Ronnie proudly pulled the medal from under my T-shirt and adjusted the red, white, and blue ribbon. He flashed it to show the Italian word PUGILATO. Oh, how he admired and loved it. Maybe even more than I did.

The waitress was impressed. Without hesitation she dashed down the counter to The Owner, and spoke in urgent, hushed whispers. He never turned around.

"I don't give a damn *who* he is!"

The voice boomed with such force that everyone's head jerked up from their plates.

"I done told you, we don't serve no niggers!"

She put her hand over her face as though she had been hit, backed up, hurried to me and began repeating the message, as though I hadn't heard it. It got real quiet.

I remember looking directly into the eyes of a white high school boy with a Manual High sweater, no older than myself, who'd been admiring my medal a minute before. Manual High was a rival school to my own Central High, and he played on the opposing teams. He looked down at the floor.

My heart was pounding. A minute before, this had been a noisy, chatty place with thirty or more customers. I pushed away from the counter. Ronnie went through every motion with me as though we'd rehearsed the act. I stood up. Knives, forks and chitchat stopped, and all eyes were on me. My mouth felt hot and dry. Never in a hundred fights did I feel blood rushing to my head as I did then.

I tried to meet the eyes of the whites along the counter, but the only eyes looking into mine were those of the old black woman from the kitchen. She came through the door, a large cross hanging from her neck, trying to get my attention by waving a small book that looked like a prayer book.

Then The Owner, arms folded, his huge stomach bulging over his apron tie, started out from around the counter as if to give me a personal message. I backed off to the centre. For an instant I had an urge to dig a right cross in the pit of his stomach, then a left hook to his mouth, then uppercut . . . and to this day I wonder if I shouldn't have obeyed that urge.

But my outlook on "fighting" had undergone a total change since the days when I scrapped in the streets and schoolyards at the slightest excuse. I had already signed for my first professional bout. It's part of the pride of a truly professional fighter not to indulge himself, not to be caught dead or alive in a free-for-all.

Most important, I had in mind another approach, one I was sure would work. I would make them feel ashamed of what they were doing. If necessary, I would stay here until they took me to jail.

I got myself together to tell them everything I'd been thinking. "This is supposed to be the land of the brave and the home of the free, and you're disgracing it with your actions. You all know me. I was born in General Hospital, only a block away. I was raised here. I went to Central High. And now I've brought back an Olympic Gold Medal for *all* the people of Louisville. I fought for the glory of my country and you should be ashamed of what you're doing. You serve any foreigner here, but not an American Negro citizen. You'll have to take me to jail, because I'll stay until I get my rights. You should be ashamed . . ."

But I never said a word.

The words wouldn't come out. Something there wouldn't let the words come out. Instead of making them feel ashamed I felt shamed. Shamed and shocked and lonesome.

The kitchen woman was wiping her face with her apron as though about to cry. The motorcycle gang had taken a sudden interest in the action, and some walked down to where The Owner was, and leaned against the counter. I saw Ronnie move his hand to his right side pocket where he kept his pearl-handled switchblade, a long, wicked weapon he'd taken off a dying pimp, "Jailhouse Sidney Green – meanest pimp I ever seen". Just as many hours as I had put in punching bags, sparring with partners and learning the art of boxing, Ronnie had spent training himself to handle his blade with frightening skill.

"You take The Owner, I take Frog," he whispered.

I shook him. In a one-on-one, two-on-one, maybe three-on-one, I could whip most of them. But the insult was so deep and painful no simple fight with fists or knives would be enough. I needed more – much more.

I had been standing there for less than a minute, but it seemed like a year. Ronnie was saying, almost in disbelief, "They don't really know who you are. They just don't know you The Champion! I ain't scared to tell 'em." Then, almost like an announcer in the ring, "Folks, this is The Champion! Louisville's Olympic Champion! Just back from Italy."

I heard my stomach growl. "Ronnie! Shut up! Don't beg. Don't beg!"

"You got sponsors," Ronnie said. "*Call* them sponsors." He reached inside my pocket for the list of the millionaires. "Go 'head. Call 'em up, tell 'em what's happening. They can buy and sell this little funky place with their pocket change. Watch their faces when Mr Viceroy tells 'em."

He gave me a dime and pushed me toward the phone on the wall.
I fumbled for the paper. An uneasy frown came on The Owner's
face.

"Don't stop, go 'head," Ronnie urged.

I was investigating the list, trying to figure which one was likely to
respond. The first name was James Ross Todd. No trouble
remembering him. Youngest of the millionaires. Only twenty-two.

Ronnie was dubious. "Chicken. Still chicken. Would he know
what to say?"

Next phone number, William Faversham, the coordinator. But he
never made a move without the others. So I went down the list.

William Lee Lyons Brown. Introduced to me as "the whiskey
billionaire" – the man who produces Jack Daniels, Old Forrester and
Early Times.

"Powerful," Ronnie approved. "Jack Daniels is powerful."

But then I remembered Mr Brown: "Boy, this makes two
generations of your family working for my family. Your mother was
a cook for my cousin." I thought of the four dollars a day they paid
Bird, and I knew I could never call him for anything under the sun.

George Washington Norton IV, millionaire oil man and horse
breeder. "A direct descendant of Martha Washington", the secretary
had whispered. "His nickname is 'Possum Norton'." I shook my
head; somehow I just couldn't call on Possum.

I moved to the next name. Patrick Calhoun, Jr., chairman of
American Commercial Barge Line. "Largest inland boat company in
the world," the secretary had said. Ronald pleaded with me to call,
so I slowly dialled his number.

No answer. I felt relieved. But Ronnie wouldn't stop: "Go on! Go
on!"

Archibald McGhee Foster. The only Northerner in the group.
Would he carry any weight down here?

"Cash, call somebody! Anybody!" Ronnie was desperate.

William Sol Cutchings. The name Ronnie wanted.

"That's him," he whispered. "He owns Viceroy and Raleigh
cigarettes! That's Brown & Williamson Tobacco Corporation. Call
him."

I strained to remember what the secretary had said. It came back
to me. "Mr Cutchings is a direct descendant of a Confederate
general," she had stated proudly. And I knew Confederate generals
had fought a civil war to keep black people in slavery. And I knew
what the Confederate flags on the jackets of the motorcycle gangs
meant. I didn't feel I could call the Confederacy.

Vertner DeGarmo Smith and Robert Worth Bingham, "millionaire newspaper publishers and TV station owners," I'd been told. But I had overheard one telling the other a darky joke and doubling up in laughter.

J. D. S. Coleman, cattle and oil tycoon. He had been the coldest of all, had thought they were paying me too much.

The last name was Elbert Gary Sutcliffe. "His people run US Steel," the secretary had said. Only because of Ronnie, I dialled US Steel's number. Finally a soft polite voice answered. "Sutcliffe residence. Yes?"

"Mr Elbert Gary Sutcliffe?" I read the name off the paper.

"Who shall I say is calling sir?"

"Cassius Clay."

Ronnie relaxed, smiling. Maybe we were getting somewhere.

After a bit, the voice of Mr Sutcliffe came over, quick, business-like, steely. "Yes, Cassius?"

"Mr Sutcliffe," I began. Then I stopped. What in the world did I want Mr Sutcliffe to do?

"Cassius? What you want?"

"Mr Sutcliffe," I started again, my throat hot and dry. There was a long pause in which I said nothing, nothing at all.

"If you want some expense money, boy, why don't you call Bill? He's the one who takes care of those things."

"Yessir, Mr Sutcliffe," and I hung up.

Ronnie looked at me in disgust. "Nigger, you didn't tell him a thing! What's wrong with you?"

What was wrong? How could I explain I could never ask Mr Sutcliffe to help me get a hamburger? I folded the letter and put it back in my pocket.

"What's wrong with you?" Ronnie kept asking.

How could I explain: my millionaires were the real rulers of Louisville. But I did not want to be considered "their" boy even in the eyes of those who hated me. I had earned my Gold Medal without their permission. It should mean something without their permission. I wanted that medallion to mean that I owned myself. And to call, seemed to me, to be exchanging one Owner for the Other. And suppose they did come to my rescue? Then I could come and go in the "white only" places, but other blacks couldn't. Then what would I be?

I moved closer to the door, keeping my eyes on The Owner. I felt a peculiar, miserable pain in my head and stomach. The pain that comes from punches you take without hitting back.

What ever illusions I'd built up in Rome as the All-American Boy were gone. My Olympic honeymoon was over. I was back in my Old Kentucky Home.

I saw The Owner relax, move behind the counter and offer Frog a cigarette. They lit up and laughed, enjoying some great joke. Before I got to the door, someone was holding my arm. The black woman from the kitchen. Close up, her face looked even thinner, her eyes larger than any eyes I'd ever seen, soft and wet and looking directly into mine.

"Son, keep the faith," she said prayerfully.

"Don't say that, lady." Ronnie looked away from her.

"Such a nice poem you wrote for our paper." She put the thin little book in my hands. The poem I wrote on the plane had appeared that week in some of the black newspapers. She had it between the pages of her little book, and I glanced at it.

HOW CASSIUS TOOK ROME
By Cassius Clay, Jr.

To make America the greatest is my goal,
So I beat the Russian, and I beat the Pole,
And for USA won the Medal of Gold.
Italians said, 'You're greater than the Cassius of Old'.
We like your name, we like your game,
So make Rome your home if you will.
I said I appreciate kind hospitality
But the USA is my country still,
'Cause they waiting to welcome me in Louisville.

It only deepened my shame, and my eyes brushed by it. Her little book was not a prayer book, but a volume of Langston Hughes poems. I put it in my pocket.

"Mary!" The Owner's voice came as though he'd caught her in treason. "Mary! In the kitchen!"

She meekly followed orders and someone began laughing and the noise and chatter returned to the restaurant. Ronnie kept up a steady stream of curses. As I pulled him outside and over to the parking lot, we heard footsteps running in the rain behind us.

"Wait! Wait!"

It was the waitress and the white boy who sat next to me at the counter. They were waving menus.

"Mr Clay, may I have your autograph?" They stood there dripping wet and panting, the rain coming down in sheets. "Please."

The boy in the Manual High sweater handed me a piece of red crayon. I scribbled "Cassius Clay – 1960" on both. They grabbed them and ran, each one in a different direction.

"Hey, Olympic nigger!"

"You still tryin' to get a milk shake?"

The voices came from the gang of motorcycle riders coming over to the lot, climbing on their hogs. Frog, one arm around his big girl friend, looked over to where we were and said. "I got your milk shake, Olympic!" They cracked up, screamed, howled, imitated Frog's gesture. Frog helped his girl onto the back of the wheel and leaned over to Kentucky Slim, apparently giving some instructions. Then, with an exaggerated gunning of the motors, they took off, *r-r-r-r-r-r-r-r-r-O-O-O-O-O-O-R-R-R-R-rrrrrrrr*, thundering past us single file, cursing, threatening, whooping.

We started our motors but sat still, our eyes on the gang. Suddenly, Kentucky broke from the pack, circled around, drove back toward us. One hand was held up like a signal and he didn't drop it until five feet from me. Ronnie moved his bike around and in between me and Kentucky.

"Clay." I can hear Slim's melancholy, nasal voice as he looked over Ronnie's shoulder. "I tried to save y'all. You done made Frog mad."

I said nothing, just waited for the real message, the settlement terms.

"Frog wanted to lynch y'all there in the restaurant," Slim confided, almost congenial. "But I said no suh. No suh! Let y'all go back where you belong, see? Just give Frog some li'l ole souvineer-like something'."

I understood exactly what he wanted, and I remember feeling tight and warm as though the bell had rung for the round.

"We fresh out of souvineers." Ronnie was cleaning his molars with a toothpick as if the restaurant had actually served him the hamburgers.

Slim pointed to my neck. "Frog wants that there ribbon and the medal for his girl. Li'l souvineer-like. And you kin go on 'bout your business." He waited. "What y'all say?"

"Slim," Ronnie said evenly, relieved the matter could be settled so simply. "Go tell Frog we give it to his mother – in trade."

Slim's mouth fell open, a bewildered, unbelieving look in his eyes. He brushed Ronnie aside to give me a reprieve. "Clay, it's yo' medal, not hisn. What you say?"

"See you later, Slim." I gunned my bike.

Flushed and furious, Slim gunned his hog, shook a prophetic

finger at me and raged, "Frog gone kill you niggers for that!" He took off, screaming back over his shoulder, "You wait! You black bastards! You wait!"

Then I knew we had already waited too long. A good many young blacks had already been caught in white neighbourhoods by this same gang, beaten, chain-whipped, some almost fatally.

If a drowning man's life parades before him when he goes down for the last time, as I had read somewhere, I was about to go under. All the years of sweat and struggle I had poured into becoming a champion flashed before me and I realized everything I wanted might go down the drain or be indefinitely delayed unless I submitted to Frog's "souvineer" hunt. A knock-down, drag-out battle with Frog's gang might leave me, if lucky enough to survive, too scarred and injured to continue as a fighter. My Gold Medal had lost its gleam in the Mayor's office and in the restaurant, but every ounce of my blood and marrow rebelled against paying it out as ransom.

I remember the rain was cold and had soaked through my sweater, down to my bones. But what made me shiver most was the awareness that in a few days my first professional fight was scheduled right here in Louisville's Freedom Hall. Against Tunney Hunsaker, a seasoned puncher who was also a police chief in Virginia. If I entered the ring with fresh cuts and scars, Hunsaker would open them.

Even though this match was made before the Louisville group entered the picture, they wanted me to drop Hunsaker and start off with an easier opponent. An old ring rule has it that a "promising amateur" must win his first professional fight if he is not to be scorned as a flash in the pan. Some commentators were not yet convinced I was for real and hopefully predicted I would be a flop against any "real professional" fighter. But I was sick of fighting "amateurs", and above all I wanted to test myself against a tough pro.

Ronnie, listening to Frog's big wheel as it circled the block, sensed what was going through my mind. "You got too much goin' for you to get messed up now."

My heart went out to him.

"I'll go on, make 'em fool with me. You get on down the other way. Go on now . . ." And he would have shoved off in Frog's direction, but I gripped his handlebars.

I had a plan. My guess was they expected me to head straight for the black neighbourhood. But I planned to get to Jefferson County

Bridge, a lonely area near rail junctions and highways, a dividing line between Kentucky and Indiana. I could cross to the Indiana side, run parallel with the river for a few miles and come back into Louisville over another bridge.

With Ronnie tight behind me, I cut across a vacant lot, shot up a side street and down an alley and for a while weaved through every intricate passageway I could find until the sound of the big motors died out.

We drove with our heads down. Straining our bikes against the wind and rain, hardly saying a word. There was no need to talk . . .

I could have phoned my policeman trainer, Joe Martin, but the thought of calling on a white Louisville policeman to help me with some white boys never entered my mind. I had known law officers in Louisville, but nothing I ever saw, heard, or experienced left me with the impression that Martin, or any white policeman, would do anything but wink if I was in trouble with his white brothers and they had the upper hand. Biographers who have described Martin as being "like a father to Cassius" don't know anything about the South, white police, and a black boy.

I remember how relieved I felt when I got within sight of the bridge. The rain had slackened, and I decided it was safe to swing from passageways and hit the bridge from Main Street.

It turned out to be a mistake. No sooner had I struck the street than I heard wild, faraway screams. "There they is! There them niggers!" A woman's high-pitched cry. "You black bastard! We got yo' ass!" Frog's bellow.

At first I could only see Frog's machine. He had apparently sent his scouts to check the route to the black neighbourhood, but he was cunning enough to suspect that I might try to get over the bridge into Indiana, and had come to seal it off. Comparing our relatively slow speed with his, and judging the distance to the bridge, it was obvious Frog would be on our backs by the time we made the top.

Ronnie leaned over, his face, like mine, wet far more from sweat than from rain. "They want you the most. Not me. You go up ahead. I'll be behind. You dig?"

I dug it. We hit the bridge and I began weaving from side to side, Ronnie dropping behind me, slightly to my right. I glanced over my shoulder, could see still another hog now, directly behind Frog. Kentucky Slim.

But Ronnie was right. Frog was almost parallel with him yet ignoring him, still concentrating on me, whirling his chain like a cowboy ready to lasso a loose steer. "Hey, Olympic nigger! So you a fighter —"

He may have said more, but with perfect timing and in a coordinated move Ronnie leaped off his machine, hurling it with all his strength underneath Frog's front wheel. Frog saw it too late, made a frantic jerk, cut to the left, skidded up against the cement mortar, smashing himself and his woman on the bridge column. The woman let out a painful scream. Badly hurt and bleeding, her blouse ripped, she scrambled over to help Frog, who hung dazed against the rail.

Kentucky was coming up behind them, whirling the same kind of chain, aiming at my head. Then and there occurred one of the two split-second moves in my life without which my career would have been forever altered. The second happened during my first championship fight with Sonny Liston, when in the fifth round, with my eyes blinded and burning from something on Liston's glove, Angelo Dundee pushed me back in the ring only a split second before the referee was about to award the fight to Liston. That incident was highly publicized. The first was here on Jefferson County Bridge.

Slim whipped his doubled-up chain at my head. Instead of slashing my face, the chain wrapped around my shoulders. Instinctively, I shot my hand out and gripped the chain and jerked with all my might. The force snatched Slim off his hog and hurled us together in a violent impact. His head struck mine and stunned me, but not enough to stop me from smashing my fist into his face. His body hit the ground, blood spurted from his nose, his empty hog careened over to the rail.

The woman was screaming, "They gonna kill Frog! They gonna kill Frog!"

Ronnie had a half nelson around Frog's neck, choking him, his blotched face even more distorted by the veins popping from his temples. The switchblade was pressed against his throat. "Get back! I'll cut his goddamn neck off! Get back!" He started ripping Frog's leather jacket as though it was tissue paper.

The girl dropped down on her knees, sobbing and pleading. Two other riders were coming up, one I remember with a flaming red, polka-dot neckpiece and a World War II German helmet.

I shouted to the girl, "Tell 'em stay off the bridge. Get 'em off the bridge!"

She sprang up, flew down to the end of the bridge, waving her arms. "Y'all go back! Go back!"

They slowed down, but kept creeping up cautiously.

"Let Frog tell 'em. Loosen up so Frog can tell 'em," I told Ronnie. He eased his grip. Frog sucked in all the breath he could, and with more force than I expected he cried out, "Y'all g'on home! G'on! G'ON!"

For a second his riders just paused at the bottom of the bridge, confused. "What you want us to do, Frog?"

The girl shouted back, "Do what Frog tells y'all! You hear? Do what he tells you!"

The rider in the German helmet pulled out what looked like a .45, and I kept my eyes on his face for the slightest flicker of what he might do. They could have overwhelmed us for certain. But just as certain they knew Ronnie would rip Frog's jugular vein.

"Lighten up," I whispered to Ronnie. Frog was our only hope. "Let Frog talk."

Frog screamed, a throaty, desperate gurgle. "I done told y'all, g'on back! G'on back home. You too, Slim! G'on!"

Slim pulled himself together like a drunkard and limped with his machine back to his battalion. They consulted briefly, looked up at us, then slowly retreated down the street. I didn't move. Just watched until I heard the girl crying. "They gone now. What you gone do with us?"

Ronnie released Frog and let him crawl over to his wheel. Like a hunter who chased what he thought would be a bunny rabbit, only to corner it and discover it to be a tiger, Frog's single thought now was escape. His girl struggled to help him mount the hog, but he kept slipping off. I stood there looking at them, feeling no anger, pity or hatred, just tension. Neither of them could ever make the hog go without our help. I moved over to the girl, and she cringed as though she expected me to hit her.

"Help us get off." She spoke very low, very desperate. "We ain't comin' back. Honest! We'll keep goin'."

I straightened the bent fenders so they wouldn't rub against the wheels, and fixed Frog's fingers on the handlebars. He was weak, unsteady, coughing as though his throat was still in Ronnie's grip. His blood, oozing through the shredded slits Ronnie's blade had made in his jacket, soaked all the way through my T-shirt as I helped him.

Ronnie and I held the hog on each side steady enough to run it down the incline and give it a mighty push. The electric starter was shot, but the hog sputtered, caught and slowly moved off, swaying a little. We watched to see if Frog would regroup the gang. But what the girl had said was true. Frog rode by them and they all fell in behind. We stood there until they disappeared, until all we could hear was rain and the shuffle and rattle of trains on the Kentucky side.

"Better get the hell away from here." Ronnie was wiping his knife on his sleeve like a violin bow. "My bike's wrecked." He surveyed what was left of it, a mass of twisted metal. Then something about my face must have stopped him. "You hurt? Goddamn – they got you?"

I shook my head. Physically, I had come off better than I expected, but the miserable pain in my head and stomach that I felt in the restaurant had returned. Give-and-take punches, like the blows exchanged with Frog's battalion, are bearable. But I was feeling the after effects of the blows I'd taken from The Owner, the Mayor, the millionaires.

"Let's wash off all this mess. You'll feel better," Ronnie concluded. We tested my bike to see if it would carry us both. "We get the blood off, we feel better."

I followed him down to the river, and hung the Olympic medal on a pier piling, the red, white and blue ribbon thick with Frog's blood. Some of it had stained the gold.

Ronnie picked it up tenderly. Even before washing himself, he washed the medal. Rubbed the lustre back into the gold, rinsed the blood off the ribbon and hung it lovingly around his own neck.

I stopped and watched. This was the first time the Gold Medal had been away from my chest since the Olympic judge hung it there that day I stood on the podium, a Russian on my left, a Pole on my right. And for the first time I saw it as it was. Ordinary, just an object. It had lost its magic. Suddenly I knew what I wanted to do with this cheap piece of metal and raggedy ribbon. And as soon as I knew, the pain in my stomach eased.

We quickly rinsed, and Ronnie put the medal back around my neck, followed me to the bridge to get the bike.

I remember thinking that the middle of the Ohio was probably the deepest part, and I walked over to the centre of the bridge. And Ronnie, with that extra sense people have who have known and loved each other for a long time, anticipated my actions. Dropping the bike, he ran toward me, yelling. But I had snapped the ribbon from around my neck. I held the medallion just far enough out so that it wouldn't tangle in the bridge structure, and threw it into the black water of the Ohio. I watched it drag the red, white and blue ribbon down to the bottom behind it.

When I turned, Ronnie had a look of horror in his eyes. "Jesus.

Oh, my God!'' Then tears came down his cheeks. "Oh, my God. You know what you did?"

"It wasn't real gold. It was phony." I tried to put my arms around him. He was wet and cold and stiff. "It was phony."

He wasn't listening. "Why you throw it in the river? Why?"

How could I put the answer together? I wasn't sure of all the reasons. The Olympic medal had been the most precious thing that had ever come to me. I worshipped it. It was proof of performance, status, a symbol of belonging, of being a part of a team, a country, a world. It was my was of redeeming myself with my teachers and schoolmates at Central High, of letting them know that although I had not won scholastic victories, there was something inside me capable of victory.

How could I explain to Ronnie I wanted something that meant more than that? Something that was as proud of me as I would be of it. Something that would let me be what I knew I had to be, my own kind of champion.

"We don't need it", I said. "We don't need it."

"You crazy fool!" He turned against me with a hostility he had never shown before. He held the neck of my sweater in a fierce grip. "They gonna let a nut like you be Champ? What you gonna tell the sponsors? They supposed to take your picture with the medal. What the papers gonna say?"

I loosened his hands from my sweater and held his arms firmly. "You won't say nothing. I won't say nothing. Nothing at all."

The medal was gone, but the sickness had gone too. I felt calm, relaxed, confident. My holiday as a White Hope was over. I felt a new, secret strength.

I tried to console Ronnie. "Wait until we win the real World Heavyweight Championship Belt." I gave him the same description an old boxing trainer had once given me of the championship belt. "That's real gold. Gold with diamonds and rubies in it. Weighs twenty pounds. The same belt handed down by Heavyweight Champions John L. Sullivan, Jack Johnson, Jess Willard, Jack Dempsey, Jack Sharkey, Max Baer, Joe Louis – a belt made for the great champions. Not phony gold."

Follow-up

1   What were Muhammad Ali's feelings about his medal, America, and his home town of Louisville when he first returned as Olympic champion?

2 What reservations did Muhammad have about the idea spread by
   the ten Louisville millionaires that they were sponsoring him
   "not for money" but out of the goodness of their hearts?
3 Why did Muhammad so bitterly regret saying to a Russian
   reporter, "Look here, Commie. America is the best country in
   the world, including yours. I'd rather live here in Louisville than
   in Africa 'cause at least I ain't fightin' off no snakes and
   alligators and livin' in mud huts"?
4 Why did Muhammad think that, on this occasion, it would
   be all right for him to eat in this particular restaurant?
5 Describe the emotions you think Muhammad experienced
   when he was refused service.
6 Imagine a similar situation in which you are involved. You
   are humiliated in some way because of your colour, your style of
   dress, your accent, or your youth. Write down the thoughts that
   swirl angrily through your mind as you struggle to make sense
   of what is happening.
7 Explain, in detail, Muhammad's reasons for throwing his gold
   medal into the Ohio river.

Down at the Cross

from an essay by James Baldwin, 1963

The essay "Down at the Cross" first appeared in the New Yorker
magazine and is currently published, along with "My Dungeon
Shook" *in his book* The Fire Next Time. *In his fiction James
Baldwin often deals with the adolescent crisis that he describes in the
extract below from the beginning of "Down at the Cross". As a
14-year-old-boy, he saw his life restricted along narrow and
conflicting paths. One path led to the safety of the church and the
other to the ways of sin that were terrifyingly evident all around him.
At fourteen he embraced the comforting safety of the church as an
escape route, but from this extract it can be seen that the church is
only a temporary refuge, ''a gimmick'', for him. In the rest of the essay*

he places white Christianity and the whole basis of white/black
relations under an exposing light.

I underwent, during the summer that I became fourteen, a
prolonged religious crisis. I use the word "religious" in the common,
and arbitrary, sense, meaning that I then discovered God, His saints
and angels, and His blazing Hell. And since I had been born in a
Christian nation, I accepted this Deity as the only one. I supposed
Him to exist only within the walls of a church – in fact, of *our*
church – and I also supposed that God and safety were synonymous.
The word "safety" brings us to the real meaning of the word
"religious" as we use it. Therefore, to state it in another, more
accurate way, I became, during my fourteenth year, for the first
time in my life, afraid – afraid of the evil within me and afraid of
the evil without. What I saw around me that summer in Harlem
was what I had always seen; nothing had changed. But now,
without any warning, the whores and pimps and racketeers on the
Avenue had become a personal menace. It had not before occurred to
me that I could become one of them, but now I realized that we had
been produced by the same circumstances. Many of my comrades
were clearly headed for the Avenue, and my father said that I was
headed that way, too. My friends began to drink and smoke, and
embarked – at first avid, then groaning – on their sexual careers.
Girls, only slightly older than I was, who sang in the choir or taught
Sunday school, the children of holy parents, underwent, before my
eyes, their incredible metamorphosis, of which the most bewildering
aspect was not their budding breasts or their rounding behinds but
something deeper and more subtle, in their eyes, their heat, their
odour, and the inflection of their voices. Like the strangers on the
Avenue, they became, in the twinkling of an eye, unutterably
different and fantastically *present*. Owing to the way I had been
raised, the abrupt discomfort that all this aroused in me and the fact
that I had no idea what my voice or my mind or my body was likely to
do next caused me to consider myself one of the most depraved
people on earth. Matters were not helped by the fact that these holy
girls seemed rather to enjoy my terrified lapses, our grim, guilty,
tormented experiments, which were at once as chill and joyless as the
Russian steppes and hotter, by far, than all the fires of Hell.

   Yet there was something deeper than these changes, and less
definable, that frightened me. It was real in both the boys and the
girls, but it was, somehow, more vivid in the boys. In the case of
girls, one watched them turning into matrons before they had

become women. They began to manifest a curious and really rather terrifying single-mindedness. It is hard to say exactly how this was conveyed: something implacable in the set of the lips, something farseeing (seeing what?) in the eyes, some new and crushing determination in the walk, something peremptory in the voice. They did not tease us, the boys, any more; they reprimanded us sharply, saying, "You better be thinking about your soul!" For the girls also saw the evidence on the Avenue, knew what the price would be for them, of one mis-step, knew that they had to be protected and that we were the only protection there was. They understood that they must act as God's decoys, saving the souls of the boys for Jesus and binding the bodies of the boys in marriage. For this was the beginning of our burning time, and "It is better," said St Paul – who elsewhere, with a most unusual and stunning exactness, described himself as a "wretched man" – "to marry than to burn." And I began to feel in the boys a curious, wary, bewildered despair, as though they were now settling in for the long, hard winter of life. I did not know then what it was that I was reacting to; I put it to myself that they were letting themselves go. In the same way that the girls were destined to gain as much weight as their mothers, the boys, it was clear, would rise no higher than their fathers. School began to reveal itself, therefore, as a child's game that one could not win, and boys dropped out of school and went to work. My father wanted me to do the same. I refused, even though I no longer had any illusions about what an education could do for me; I had already encountered too many college-graduate handymen. My friends were now "downtown", busy, as they put it, "fighting the man". They began to care less about the way they looked, the way they dressed, the things they did; presently, one found them in twos and threes and fours, in a hallway, sharing a jug of wine or a bottle of whiskey, talking, cursing, fighting, sometimes weeping: lost, and unable to say what it was that oppressed them, except that they knew it was "the man" – the white man. And there seemed to be no way whatever to remove this cloud that stood between them and the sun, between them and love and life and power, between them and whatever it was that they wanted. One did not have to be very bright to realize how little one could do to change one's situation; one did not have to be abnormally sensitive to be worn down to a cutting edge by the incessant and gratuitous humiliation and danger one encountered every working day, all day long. The humiliation did not apply merely to working days, or workers; I was thirteen and was crossing Fifth Avenue on my way to the Forty-second

Street library, and the cop in the middle of the street muttered as I passed him, "Why don't you niggers stay uptown where you belong?" When I was ten, and didn't look, certainly, any older, two policemen amused themselves with me by frisking me, making comic (and terrifying) speculations concerning my ancestry and probable sexual prowess and, for good measure, leaving me flat on my back in one of Harlem's empty lots. Just before and then during the Second World War, many of my friends fled into the service, all to be changed there, and rarely for the better, many to be ruined, and many to die. Others fled to other states and cities – that is, to other ghettos. Some went on wine or whiskey or the needle, and are still on it. And others, like me, fled into the church.

For the wages of sin were visible everywhere, in every wine-stained and urine-splashed hallway, in every clanging ambulance bell, in every scar on the faces of the pimps and their whores, in every helpless, new-born baby being brought into this danger, in every knife and pistol fight on the Avenue, and in every disastrous bulletin: a cousin, mother of six, suddenly gone mad, the children parcelled out here and there; an indestructible aunt rewarded for years of hard labour by a slow, agonizing death in a terrible small room; someone's bright son blown into eternity by his own hand; another turned robber and carried off to jail. It was a summer of dreadful speculations and discoveries, of which these were not the worst. Crime became real, for example – for the first time – not as a possibility but as *the* possibility. One would never defeat one's circumstances by working and saving one's pennies; one would never, by working, acquire that many pennies and, besides, the social treatment accorded even the most successful Negroes proved that one needed, in order to be free, something more than a bank account. One needed a handle, a lever, a means of inspiring fear. It was absolutely clear that the police would whip you and take you in as long as they could get away with it, and that everyone else – housewives, taxi-drivers, elevator boys, dishwashers, bartenders, lawyers, judges, doctors, and grocers – would never by the operation of any generous human feeling, cease to use you as an outlet for his frustrations and hostilities. Neither civilized reason nor Christian love would cause any of those people to treat you as they presumably wanted to be treated; only the fear of your power to retaliate would cause them to do that, or to seem to do it, which was (and is) good enough. There appears to be a vast amount of confusion on this point, but I do not know many Negroes who are eager to be "accepted" by white people, still less to be loved by them; they, the blacks, simply don't wish to be beaten over the head by the whites every instant of our brief passage on this planet. White people in this country will have quite enough to do in learning how to accept and love themselves and each other, and when they have achieved this – which will not be tomorrow and may very well be never – the Negro problem will no longer exist, for it will no longer be needed.

People more advantageously placed than we in Harlem were, and are, will no doubt find the psychology and the view of human nature sketched above dismal and shocking in the extreme. But the Negro's experience of the white world cannot possibly create in him any respect for the standards by which the white world claims to live. His own condition is overwhelming proof that white people do not live by these standards. Negro servants have been smuggling odds and ends out of white homes for generations, and white people have been delighted to have them do it, because it has assuaged a dim guilt and testified to the intrinsic superiority of white people. Even the most doltish and servile Negro could scarcely fail to be impressed by the disparity between his situation and that of the people for whom he worked; Negroes who were neither doltish nor servile did not feel that they were doing anything wrong when they robbed white people. In spite of the Puritan–Yankee equation of virtue with well-being, Negroes had excellent reasons for doubting that money was made or kept by any very striking adherence to the Christian virtues; it certainly did not work that way for black Christians. In any case, white people, who had robbed black people of their liberty and who profited by this theft every hour that they lived, had no moral ground on which to stand. They had the judges, the juries, the shotguns, the law – in a word, power. But it was a criminal power, to be feared but not respected, and to be outwitted in any way whatever. And those virtues preached but not practised by the white world were merely another means of holding Negroes in subjection.

It turned out, then, that summer, that the moral barriers that I had supposed to exist between me and the dangers of a criminal career were so tenuous as to be nearly non-existent. I certainly could not discover any principled reason for not becoming a criminal, and it is not my poor, God-fearing parents who are to be indicted for the lack, but this society. I was icily determined – more determined, really, than I then knew – never to make my peace with the ghetto but to die and go to Hell before I would let any white man spit on me, before I would accept my "place" in this republic. I did not intend to allow the white people of this country to tell me who I was, and limit me that way, and polish me off that way. And yet, of course, at the same time, I *was* being spat on and defined and described and limited, and could have been polished off with no effort whatever. Every Negro boy – in my situation during those years, at least – who reaches this point realizes, at once, profoundly, because he wants to live, that he stands in great peril and must find, with speed, a "thing", a gimmick, to lift him out, to start him on his way. *And it does not matter what the gimmick is.* It was this last realization that terrified me and – since it revealed that the door opened on so many dangers – helped to hurl me into the church. And, by an unforeseeable paradox, it was my career in the church that turned out, precisely, to be my gimmick.

Follow-up

1   What reasons does James Baldwin give for the "curious, wary, bewildered despair" that he begins to feel in the boys who were his friends and acquaintances?
2   What examples does he give of the "gratuitous humiliation" that blacks could receive? Into what sort of lives does this constant oppression lead them?
3   What reasons does he give for the white man's callous treatment of the black man?
4   Describe in detail what causes him, when he has assessed the situation around him, to choose the church as an escape route.

Fighting Back

Racism in America still exists, but at least today racist behaviour is often acknowledged as such by large sections of American society, both white and black, and it is fought against in a determined and organized way. A great deal of credit for this change in attitude must go to two black Americans who rose to prominence in the 1960s, Martin Luther King through peaceful protest, and Malcolm X through advocating more violent action, forged movements of solidarity from the strands of black resistance that had been simmering and forced white America to reconsider. "Black is Beautiful" was one rallying cry and "We shall Overcome" another. In the following story and extracts, the strength of that desire to overcome is made clearly evident.

Little Man Grows Up

from *Roll of Thunder, Hear my Cry* by Mildred D. Taylor, 1976

*Roll of Thunder, Hear My Cry is a book about growing up in
the Mississippi of the 1930s. It is narrated by a young girl, Cassie
Logan, who, as she grows up, gradually learns about the oppressive
tensions that exist between black and white people.*

*She experiences humiliation and she experiences terror as a result
of this racial hatred but, surrounded by a strong and loving family,
she learns to define for herself what is important and what she is
going to fight for. It is an inspiring story.*

*In this extract from near the beginning of the book, Cassie arrives
back in school after a holiday with her brothers Stacey, Christopher-
John and Little Man and their friends T.J. and Claude. She is soon
involved in backing her little brother's stand against second-class
treatment.*

The Great Faith Elementary and Secondary School, one of the
largest black schools in the county, was a dismal end to an hour's
journey. Consisting of four weather-beaten wooden houses on stilts
of brick, 320 students, seven teachers, a principal, a caretaker, and
the caretaker's cow, which kept the wide crabgrass lawn sufficiently
clipped in spring and summer, the school was located near three
plantations, the largest and closest by far being the Granger
plantation. Most of the students were from families that
sharecropped on Granger land, and the others mainly from Montier
and Harrison plantation families. Because the students were needed
in the fields from early spring when the cotton was planted until
after most of the cotton had been picked in the fall, the school
adjusted its terms accordingly, beginning in October and dismissing
in March. But even so, after today a number of the older students
would not be seen again for a month or two, not until the last puff
of cotton had been gleaned from the fields, and eventually most
would drop out of school altogether. Because of this, the classes in
the higher grades grew smaller with each passing year.

The class buildings, with their backs practically against the forest
wall, formed a semicircle facing a small one-room church at the
opposite edge of the compound. It was to this church that many of
the school's students and their parents belonged. As we arrived, the
enormous iron bell in the church belfry was ringing vigorously,

warning the milling students that only five minutes of freedom remained.

Little Man immediately pushed his way across the lawn to the well. Stacey and T.J., ignoring the rest of us now that they were on the school grounds, wandered off to be with the other seventh-grade boys, and Christopher-John and Claude rushed to reunite with their classmates of last year. Left alone, I dragged slowly to the building that held the first four grades and sat on the bottom step. Plopping my pencils and notebook into the dirt, I propped my elbows on my knees and rested my chin in the palms of my hands.

"Hey, Cassie," said Mary Lou Wellever, the principal's daughter, as she flounced by in a new yellow dress.

"Hey, yourself," I said, scowling so ferociously that she kept on walking. I stared after her a moment noting that she *would* have on a new dress. Certainly no one else did. Patches on faded pants and dresses abounded on boys and girls come so recently from the heat of the cotton fields. Girls stood awkwardly, afraid to sit, and boys pulled restlessly at starched, high-buttoned collars. Those students fortunate enough to have shoes hopped from one pinched foot to the other. Tonight the Sunday clothes would be wrapped in newspaper and hung for Sunday and the shoes would be packed away to be brought out again only when the weather turned so cold that bare feet could no longer traverse the frozen roads; but for today we all suffered.

On the far side of the lawn I spied Moe Turner speeding toward the seventh-grade-class building, and wondered at his energy. Moe was one of Stacey's friends. He lived on the Montier plantation, a three-and-a-half-hour walk from the school. Because of the distance, many children from the Montier plantation did not come to Great Faith after they had finished the four-year school near Smellings Creek. But there were some girls and boys like Moe who made the trek daily, leaving their homes while the sky was black and not returning until all was blackness again. I for one was certainly glad that I didn't live that far away. I don't think my feet would have wanted that badly for me to be educated.

The chiming of the second bell began. I stood up dusting my bottom as the first, second, third, and fourth graders crowded up the stairs into the hallway. Little Man flashed proudly past, his face and hands clean and his black shoes shining again. I glanced down at my own shoes powdered red and, raising my right foot, rubbed it against the back of my left leg, then reversed the procedure. As the last gong of the bell reverberated across the compound, I swooped up my pencils and notebook and ran inside.

A hallway extended from the front to the back door of the building. On either side of the hallway were two doorways, both leading into the same large room which was divided into two classrooms by a heavy canvas-curtain. The second and third grades were on the left, the first and fourth grades on the right. I hurried to the rear of the building, turned to the right, and slid into a third-row bench occupied my Gracey Pearson and Alma Scott.

"You can't sit here," objected Gracey. "I'm saving it for Mary Lou."

I glanced back at Mary Lou Wellever, depositing her lunch pail on a shelf in the back of the room and said, "Not any more you ain't."

Miss Daisy Crocker, yellow and buckeyed, glared down at me from the middle of the room with a look that said, "Soooooooo, it's you, Cassie Logan." Then she pursed her lips and drew the curtain along the rusted iron rod and tucked it into a wide loop in the back wall. With the curtain drawn back, the first graders gazed quizzically at us. Little Man sat by a window, his hands folded, patiently waiting for Miss Crocker to speak.

Mary Lou nudged me. "That's my seat, Cassie Logan."

"Mary Lou Wellever," Miss Crocker called primly, "Have a seat."

"Yes, ma'am," said Mary Lou, eyeing me with a look of pure hate before turning away.

Miss Crocker walked stiffly to her desk, which was set on a tiny platform and piled high with bulky objects covered by a tarpaulin. She rapped the desk with a ruler, although the room was perfectly still, and said, "Welcome, children, to Great Faith Elementary School." Turning slightly so that she stared squarely at the left side of the room, she continued, "To all of you fourth graders, it's good to have you in my class. I'll be expecting many good and wonderful things from you." Then, addressing the right side of the room, she said, "And to all our little first grade friends only today starting on the road to knowledge and education, may your tiny feet find the pathways of learning steady and forever before you."

Already bored, I stretched my right arm on the desk and rested my head in my upraised hand.

Miss Crocker smiled mechanically, then rapped on her desk again. "Now, little ones," she said, still talking to the first grade, "your teacher, Miss Davis, has been held up in Jackson for a few days so I'll have the pleasure of sprinkling your little minds with the first rays of knowledge." She beamed down upon them as if she expected to be applauded for this bit of news, then with a swoop of her large eyes to include the fourth graders, she went on.

"Now since there's only one of me, we shall have to sacrifice for the next few days. We shall work, work, work, but we shall have to work like little Christian boys and girls and share, share, share. Now are we willing to do that?"

"YES'M, MIZ CROCKER," the children chorused.

But I remained silent. I never did approve of group responses. Adjusting my head in my hand, I sighed heavily, my mind on the burning of the Berrys.

"Cassie Logan?"

I looked up, startled.

"Cassie Logan!"

"Yes, ma'am?" I jumped up quickly to face Miss Crocker.

"Aren't you willing to work and share?"

"Yes'm."

"Then say so!"

"Yes'm," I murmured, sliding back into my seat as Mary Lou, Gracey, and Alma giggled. Here it was only five minutes into the new school year and already I was in trouble.

By ten o'clock, Miss Crocker had rearranged our seating and written our names on her seating chart. I was still sitting beside Gracey and Alma but we had been moved from the third to the first row in front of a small potbellied stove. Although being eyeball to eyeball with Miss Crocker was nothing to look forward to, the prospect of being warm once the cold weather set in was nothing to be sneezed at either, so I resolved to make the best of my rather dubious position.

Now Miss Crocker made a startling announcement: This year we would all have books.

Everyone gasped, for most of the students had never handled a book at all besides the family Bible. I admit that even I was somewhat excited. Although Mama had several books, I had never had one of my very own.

"Now we're very fortunate to get these readers," Miss Crocker explained while we eagerly awaited the unveiling. "The county superintendent of schools himself brought these books down here for our use and we must take extra-good care of them." She moved toward her desk. "So let's all promise that we'll take the best care possible of these new books." She stared down, expecting our response. "All right, all together, let's repeat, 'We promise to take good care of our new books.'" She looked sharply at me as she spoke.

"WE PROMISE TO TAKE GOOD CARE OF OUR NEW BOOKS!"

"Fine," Miss Crocker beamed, then proudly threw back the tarpaulin.

Sitting so close to the desk, I could see that the covers of the books, a motley red, were badly worn and that the grey edges of the pages had been marred by pencils, crayons, and ink. My anticipation at having my own book ebbed to a sinking disappointment. But Miss Crocker continued to beam as she called each fourth grader to her desk and, recording a number in her roll book, handed him or her a book.

As I returned from my trip to her desk, I noticed the first graders anxiously watching the disappearing pile. Miss Crocker must have noticed them too, for as I sat down she said, "Don't worry, little ones, there are plenty of readers for you too. See there on Miss Davis's desk." Wide eyes turned to the covered teacher's platform directly in front of them and an audible sigh of relief swelled in the room.

I glanced across at Little Man, his face lit in eager excitement. I knew that he could not see the soiled covers or the marred pages from where he sat, and even though his penchant for cleanliness was often annoying, I did not like to think of his disappointment when he saw the books as they really were. But there was nothing that I could do about it, so I opened my book to its centre and began browsing through the spotted pages. Girls with blond braids and boys with blue eyes stared up at me. I found a story about a boy and his dog lost in a cave and began reading while Miss Crocker's voice droned on monotonously.

Suddenly I grew conscious of a break in that monotonous tone and I looked up. Miss Crocker was sitting at Miss Davis's desk with the first-grade books stacked before her, staring fiercely down at Little Man, who was pushing a book back upon the desk.

"What's that you said, Clayton Chester Logan?" she asked.

The room became gravely silent. Everyone knew that Little Man was in big trouble for no one, but no one, ever called Little Man "Clayton Chester" unless she or he meant serious business.

Little Man knew this too. His lips parted slightly as he took his hands from the book. He quivered, but he did not take his eyes from Miss Crocker. "I – I said may I have another book please, ma'am," he squeaked. "That one's dirty."

"Dirty!" Miss Crocker echoed, appalled by such temerity. She stood up, gazing down upon Little Man like a bony giant, but Little Man raised his head and continued to look into her eyes. "Dirty!

And just who do you think you are, Clayton Chester? Here the county is giving us these wonderful books during these hard times and you're going to stand there and tell me that the book's too dirty? Now you take that book or get nothing at all!"

Little Man lowered his eyes and said nothing as he stared at the book. For several moments he stood there, his face barely visible above the desk, then he turned and looked at the few remaining books and, seeming to realize that they were as badly soiled as the one Miss Crocker had given him, he looked across the room at me. I nodded and Little Man, glancing up again at Miss Crocker, slid the book from the edge of the desk, and with his back straight and his head up returned to his seat.

Miss Crocker sat down again. "Some people around here seem to be giving themselves airs. I'll tolerate no more of that," she scowled. "Sharon Lake, come get your book."

I watched Little Man as he scooted into his seat beside two other little boys. He sat for a while with a stony face looking out the window; then, evidently accepting the fact that the book in front of him was the best that he could expect, he turned and opened it. But as he stared at the book's inside cover, his face clouded, changing from sulky acceptance to puzzlement. His brows furrowed. Then his eyes grew wide, and suddenly he sucked in his breath and sprang from his chair like a wounded animal, flinging the book onto the floor and stomping madly upon it.

Miss Crocker rushed to Little Man and grabbed him up in powerful hands. She shook him vigorously, then set him on the floor again. "Now, just what's gotten into you, Clayton Chester?"

But Little Man said nothing. He just stood staring down at the open book, shivering with indignant anger.

"Pick it up," she ordered.

"No!" defied Little Man.

"No? I'll give you ten seconds to pick up that book, boy, or I'm going to get my switch."

Little Man bit his lower lip, and I knew that he was not going to pick up the book. Rapidly, I turned to the inside cover of my own book and saw immediately what had made Little Man so furious. Stamped on the inside cover was a chart which read:

PROPERTY OF THE BOARD OF EDUCATION

Spokane County, Mississippi

September, 1922

CHRONOLOGICAL ISSUANCE	DATE OF ISSUANCE	CONDITION OF BOOK	RACE OF STUDENT
1	September 1922	New	White
2	September 1923	Excellent	White
3	September 1924	Excellent	White
4	September 1925	Very Good	White
5	September 1926	Good	White
6	September 1927	Good	White
7	September 1928	Average	White
8	September 1929	Average	White
9	September 1930	Average	White
10	September 1931	Poor	White
11	September 1932	Poor	White
12	September 1933	Very Poor	nigra
13			
14			
15			

The blank lines continued down to line 20 and I knew that they had all been reserved for black students. A knot of anger swelled in my throat and held there. But as Miss Crocker directed Little Man to bend over the "whipping" chair, I put aside my anger and jumped up.

"Miz Crocker, don't, please!" I cried. Miss Crocker's dark eyes warned me not to say another word. "I know why he done it!"

"You want part of this switch, Cassie?"

"No'm," I said hastily. "I just wanna tell you how come Little Man done what he done."

"Sit down!" she ordered as I hurried toward her with the open book in my hand.

Holding the book up to her, I said, "See, Miz Crocker, see what it says. They give us these ole books when they didn't want 'em no more."

She regarded me impatiently, but did not look at the book. "Now how could he know what it says? He can't read."

"Yes'm, he can. He been reading since he was four. He can't read all them big words, but he can read them columns. See what's in the last row. Please look, Miz Crocker."

This time Miss Crocker did look, but her face did not change. Then, holding up her head, she gazed unblinkingly down at me.

"S'see what they called us," I said, afraid she had not seen.

"That's what you are," she said coldly. "Now go sit down."

I shook my head, realizing now that Miss Crocker did not even know what I was talking about. She had looked at the page and had understood nothing.

"I said sit down, Cassie!"

I started slowly toward my desk, but as the hickory stick sliced the tense air, I turned back around. "Miz Crocker," I said, "I don't want my book neither."

The switch landed hard upon Little Man's upturned bottom. Miss Crocker looked questioningly at me as I reached up to her desk and placed the book upon it. Then she swung the switch five more times and, discovering that Little Man had no intention of crying, ordered him up.

"All right, Cassie," she sighed, turning to me, "come on and get yours."

By the end of the school day I had decided that I would tell Mama everything before Miss Crocker had a chance to do so. From nine years of trial and error, I had learned that punishment was always less severe when I poured out the whole truth to Mama on my own before she had heard anything from anyone else. I knew that Miss Crocker had not spoken to Mama during the lunch period, for she had spent the whole hour in the classroom preparing for the afternoon session.

As soon as class was dismissed I sped from the room, weaving a path through throngs of students happy to be free. But before I could reach the seventh-grade-class building, I had the misfortune to collide with Mary Lou's father. Mr Wellever looked down on me with surprise that I would actually bump into him, then proceeded to lecture me on the virtues of watching where one was going. Meanwhile Miss Crocker briskly crossed the lawn to Mama's class

building. By the time I escaped Mr Wellever, she had already
disappeared into the darkness of the hallway.

Mama's classroom was in the back. I crept silently along the quiet
hall and peeped cautiously into the open doorway. Mama, pushing a
strand of her long, crinkly hair back into the chignon at the base of
her slender neck, was seated at her desk watching Miss Crocker thrust
a book before her. "Just look at that, Mary," Miss Crocker said, thump-
ing the book twice with her forefinger. "A perfectly good book ruined.
Look at that broken binding and those foot marks all over it."

Mama did not speak as she studied the book.

"And here's the one Cassie wouldn't take," she said, placing a
second book on Mama's desk with an outraged slam. "At least she
didn't have a tantrum and stomp all over hers. I tell you, Mary, I
just don't know what got into those children today. I always knew
Cassie was rather high-strung, but Little Man! He's always such a
perfect little gentleman."

Mama glanced at the book I had rejected and opened the front
cover so that the offensive pages of both books faced her. "You say
Cassie said it was because of this front page that she and Little Man
didn't want the books?" Mama asked quietly.

"Yes, ain't that something?" Miss Crocker said, forgetting her
teacher-training-school diction in her indignation. "The very idea!
That's on all the books, and why they got so upset about it I'll
never know."

"You punish them?" asked Mama, glancing up at Miss Crocker.

"Well, I certainly did! Whipped both of them good with my
hickory stick. Wouldn't you have?" When Mama did not reply, she
added defensively, "I had a perfect right to."

"Of course you did, Daisy," Mama said, turning back to the
books again. "They disobeyed you." But her tone was so quiet and
noncommittal that I knew Miss Crocker was not satisfied with her
reaction.

"Well, I thought you would've wanted to know, Mary, in case you
wanted to give them a piece of your mind also."

Mama smiled up at Miss Crocker and said rather absently, "Yes, of
course, Daisy. Thank you." Then she opened her desk drawer and
pulled out some paper, a pair of scissors and a small brown bottle.

Miss Crocker, dismayed by Mama's seeming unconcern for the
seriousness of the matter, thrust her shoulders back and began
moving away from the desk. "You understand that if they don't
have those books to study from, I'll have to fail them in both reading
and composition, since I plan to base all my lessons around –." She

stopped abruptly and stared in amazement at Mama. "Mary, what in the world are you doing?"

Mama did not answer. She had trimmed the paper to the size of the books and was now dipping a grey-looking glue from the brown bottle onto the inside cover of one of the books. Then she took the paper and placed it over the glue.

"Mary Logan, do you know what you're doing? That book belongs to the county. If somebody from the superintendent's office ever comes down here and sees that book, you'll be in real trouble."

Mama laughed and picked up the other book. "In the first place no one cares enough to come down here, and in the second place if anyone should come, maybe he could see all the things we need — current books for all of our subjects, not just somebody's old throwaways, desks, paper, blackboards, erasers, maps, chalk . . ." Her voice trailed off as she glued the second book.

"Biting the hand that feeds you. That's what you're doing, Mary Logan, biting the hand that feeds you."

Again, Mama laughed. "If that's the case, Daisy, I don't think I need that little bit of food." With the second book finished, she stared at a small pile of seventh-grade books on her desk.

"Well, I just think you're spoiling those children. Mary. They've got to learn how things are sometime."

"Maybe so," Mama said, "but that doesn't mean they have to accept them . . . and maybe we don't either."

Miss Crocker gazed suspiciously at Mama. Although Mama had been a teacher at Great Faith for fourteen years, ever since she had graduated from the Crandon Teacher Training School at nineteen, she was still considered by many of the other teachers as a disrupting maverick. Her ideas were always a bit too radical and her statements a bit too pointed. The fact that she had not grown up in Spokane County but in the Delta made her even more suspect, and the more traditional thinkers like Miss Crocker were wary of her.

"Well, if anyone ever does come from the county and sees Cassie's and Little Man's books messed up like that," she said, "I certainly won't accept the responsibility for them."

"It will be easy enough for anyone to see whose responsibility it is, Daisy, by opening any seventh-grade book. Because tomorrow I'm going to 'mess them up' too."

Miss Crocker, finding nothing else to say, turned imperiously and headed for the door. I dashed across the hall and awaited her exit, then crept back.

Mama remained at her desk, sitting very still. For a long time she did not move. When she did, she picked up one of the seventh-grade books and began to glue again. I wanted to go and help her, but something warned me that now was not the time to make my presence known, and I left.

I would wait until the evening to talk to her; there was no rush now. She understood.

Follow-up

1   What evidence is there in this extract of some of the children's great desire to continue their education?
2   Write down all you learn about Cassie Logan's personality.
3   Make a list of all the reasons why Little Man refuses to accept his book.
4   What is the difference in attitude of Miss Crocker and Mary Logan, the children's mother, to the episode of the textbooks?
5   Write a story about standing up for your rights in the face of authority. It could, for example be about the way you dress or the length of your hair.

The Convert

A short story by Lerone Bennett Jr., 1963

What makes the fighting back in The Convert *so moving and so significant is that the freedom fighters are not hot-headed young revolutionaries but respectable men who have carved a comfortable niche for themselves within the limits of the American society in the 1960s. Both men realize in late middle age that there is something more than wealth and respectability that they must hand over to their sons.*

A man don't know what he'll do, a man don't know what he is till he gets his back pressed up against a wall. Now you take Aaron Lott: there ain't no other way to explain the crazy thing he did. He was going along fine, preaching the gospel, saving souls, and getting along with the white folks; and then, all of a sudden, he felt wood pressing against his back. The funny thing was that nobody knew he was hurting till he preached that Red Sea sermon where he got mixed up and seemed to think Mississippi was Egypt. As chairman of the deacon's board, I felt it was my duty to reason with him. I appreciated his position and told him so, but I didn't think it was right for him to push us all in a hole. The old fool – he just laughed.

"Brother Booker," he said, "the Lord – He'll take care of me."

I knew then that that man was heading for trouble. And the very next thing he did confirmed it. The white folks called the old fool downtown to bear witness that the coloured folks were happy. And you know what he did: he got down there amongst all them big white folks and he said: "Things ain't gonna change here overnight, but they gonna change. It's inevitable. The Lord wants it."

Well sir, you could have bought them white folks for a penny. Aaron Lott, pastor of the Rock of Zion Baptist Church, a man white folks had said was wise and sound and sensible, had come close – too close – to saying that the Supreme Court was coming to Melina, Mississippi. The surprising thing was that the white folks didn't do nothing. There was a lot of mumbling and whispering, but nothing bad happened till the terrible morning when Aaron came a-knocking at the door of my funeral home. Now things had been tightening up – you could feel it in the air – and I didn't want no part of no crazy scheme, and I told him so right off. He walked on past me and sat down on the couch. He had on his preaching clothes, a shiny blue suit, a fresh starched white shirt, a black tie, and his Sunday black shoes. I remember thinking at the time that Aaron was too black to be wearing all them dark clothes. The thought tickled me, and I started to smile, but then I noticed something about him that didn't seem quite right. I ran my eyes over him closely. He was kinda middle-sized and he had a big clean-shaven head, a big nose, and thin lips. I stood there looking at him for a long time, but I couldn't figure out what it was till I looked at his eyes: they were burning bright, like light bulbs do just before they go out. And yet he looked contented, like his mind was resting somewheres else.

"I wanna talk with you, Booker," he said, glancing sideways at my wife. "If you don't mind, Sister Brown –"

Sarah got up and went into the living quarters. Aaron didn't say nothing for a long time; he just sat there looking out the window. Then he spoke so soft I had to strain my ears to hear.

"I'm leaving for the Baptist convention," he said. He pulled out his gold watch and looked at it. "Train leaves in 'bout two hours."

"I know *that*, Aaron."

"Yeah, but what I wanted to tell you was that I ain't going Jim Crow. I'm going first class, Booker, right through the white waiting room. That's the law."

A cold shiver ran through me.

"Aaron," I said, "don't you go talking crazy now."

The old fool laughed, a great big body-shaking laugh. He started talking 'bout God and Jesus and all that stuff. Now, I'm a God-fearing man myself, but I holds that God helps those who help themselves. I told him so.

"You can't mix God up with these white folks," I said. "When you start to messing around with segregation, they'll burn you up and the Bible, too."

He looked at me like I was Satan.

"I sweated over this thing," he said. "I prayed. I got down on my knees, and I asked God not to give me this cup. But He said I was the one. I heard Him, Booker, right here (he tapped his chest) in my heart."

The old fool's been having visions, I thought. I sat down and tried to figure out a way to hold him, but he got up, without saying a word, and started for the door.

"Wait!" I shouted, "I'll get my coat."

"I don't need you," he said. "I just came by to tell you so you could tell the board in case something happened."

"You wait," I shouted, and ran out of the room to get my coat.

We got in his beat-up old Ford and went by the parsonage to get his suitcase. Rachel – that was his wife – and Jonah were sitting in the living room, wringing their hands. Aaron got his bag, shook Jonah's hand, and said, "Take care of your Mamma, boy." Jonah nodded. Aaron hugged Rachel and pecked at her cheek. Rachel broke down. She throwed her arms around his neck and carried on something awful. Aaron shoved her away.

"Don't go making no fuss over it, woman. I ain't gonna be gone forever. Can't a man go to a church meeting 'thout women screaming and crying."

He tried to make light of it, but you could see he was touched by the way his lips trembled. He held his hand out to me, but I wouldn't take it. I told him off good, told him it was a sin and a shame for a man of God to be carrying on like he was, worrying his wife and everything.

"I'm coming with you," I said. "Somebody's gotta see that you don't make a fool of yourself."

He shrugged, picked up his suitcase, and started for the door. Then he stopped and turned around and looked at his wife and his boy, and from the way he looked I knew that there was still a chance. He looked at the one and then at the other. For a moment there, I thought he was going to cry, but he turned, quick-like, and walked out of the door.

I ran after him and tried to talk some sense in his head but he shook me off, turned the corner, and went on up Adams Street. I caught up with him, and we walked in silence, crossing the street in front of the First Baptist Church for whites, going on around the Confederate monument where, once, they hung a boy for fooling around with white women.

"Put it off, Aaron," I begged. "Sleep on it."

He didn't say nothing.

"What you need is a vacation. I'll get the board to approve, full pay and everything."

He smiled and shifted the suitcase over to his left hand. Big drops of sweat were running down his face and spotting up his shirt. His eyes were awful, all lit up and burning.

"Aaron, Aaron, can't you hear me?"

We passed the feed store, Bill Williams' grocery store, and the movie house.

"A man's gotta think about his family, Aaron. A man ain't free. Didn't you say that once, didn't you?"

He shaded his eyes with his hand and looked into the sun. He put the suitcase on the ground and checked his watch.

"Why don't you think about Jonah?" I asked. "Answer that. Why don't you think about your own son?"

"I am," he said. "That's exactly what I'm doing, thinking about Jonah. Matter of fact, he started *me* to thinking. I ain't never mentioned it before, but the boy's been worrying me. One day we was downtown here, and he asked me something that hurt. 'Daddy,' he said, 'how come you ain't a man?' I got mad. I did, and told him: 'I am a man.' He said that wasn't what he meant. 'I mean,' he said, 'how come you ain't a man where white folks concerned.' I couldn't answer him, Booker. I'll never forget it till the day I die. I couldn't answer my own son, and I been preaching forty years."

"He don't know nothing 'bout it," I said. "He's hot-headed, like my boy. He'll find out when he grows up."

"I hopes not," Aaron said, shaking his head. "I hopes not."

Some white folks passed, and we shut up till they were out of hearing. Aaron, who was acting real strange, looked up in the sky and moved his lips. He came back to himself after a little bit, and he said: "This thing of being a man, Booker, is a big thing. The Supreme Court can't make you a man. The NAACP can't do it. God Almighty can do a lot, but even He can't do it. Ain't nobody can do it but you."

He said that like he was preaching, and when he got through, he was all filled up with emotion, and he seemed kind of ashamed – he was a man who didn't like emotion outside the church. He looked at his watch, picked up his bag, and said, "Well, let's git it over with."

We turned into Elm, and the first thing I saw at the end of the street was the train station. It was an old red building, flat like a slab. A group of white men were fooling around in front of the door. I couldn't make them out from that distance, but I could tell they weren't the kind of white folks to be fooling around with.

We walked on, passing the dry goods store, the barber shop, and the new building that was going up. Across the street from that was the sheriff's office. I looked in the window and saw Bull Sampson sitting at his desk, his feet propped up on a chair, a fat brown cigar sticking out of his mouth. A ball about the size of a sweet potato started burning in my stomach.

"Please Aaron," I said. "Please. You can't get away with it, I know how you feel. Sometimes I feel the same way myself, but I wouldn't risk my neck to do nothing for these people. They won't appreciate it; they'll laugh at you."

We were almost to the station and I could make out the faces of the men sitting on the benches. One of them must have been telling a joke. He finished, and the group broke out laughing.

I whispered to Aaron: "I'm through with it. I wash my hands of the whole mess."

I don't know whether he heard me or not. He turned to the right without saying a word and went on in the front door. The string-beany man who told the joke was so shocked that his cigarette fell out of his mouth.

"Y'all see that," he said. "Why, I'll –"

"Shut up," another man said. "Go git Bull."

I kept walking, fast, turned the corner, and ran around to the coloured waiting room. When I got in there, I looked through the ticket window and saw Aaron standing in front of the clerk. Aaron stood there for a minute or more, but the clerk didn't see him. And that took some not seeing. In that room Aaron Lott stood out like a pig in a chicken coop.

There were, I'd say, about ten or fifteen people in there, but didn't none of them move. They just sat there with their eyes glued on Aaron's back. Aaron cleared his throat. The clerk didn't look up; he got real busy with some papers. Aaron cleared his throat again and opened his mouth to speak. The screen door of the waiting room opened and clattered shut.

It got real quiet in that room, hospital quiet. It got so quiet I could hear my own heart beating. Now Aaron knew who opened that door, but he didn't bat an eyelid. He turned around real slow and faced High Sheriff Sampson, the baddest man in South Mississippi.

Mr Sampson stood there with his legs wide open, like the men you see on television. His beefy face was blood-red, and his grey eyes were rattlesnake hard. He was mad; no doubt about it. I had never seen him so mad.

"Preacher," he said, "you done gone crazy?" He was talking low-like and mean.

"Nosir," Aaron said. "Nosir, Mr Sampson."

"What you think you doing?"

"Going to St Louis, Mr Sampson."

"You must done lost yo' mind, boy."

Mr Sampson started walking toward Aaron with his hand on his gun. Twenty or thirty men pushed through the front door and fanned out over the room. Mr Sampson stopped about two paces from Aaron and looked him up an down. That look had paralysed hundreds of niggers; but it didn't faze Aaron none – he stood his ground.

"I'm gonna give you a chance, preacher. Git on over to the nigger side and git quick."

"I ain't bothering nobody, Mr Sampson."

Somebody in the crowd yelled: "Don't reason wit' the nigger, Bull. Hit 'im."

Mr Sampson walked up to Aaron and grabbed him in the collar and throwed him up against the ticket counter. He pulled out his gun.

"Did you hear me, deacon. I said, 'Git.'"

"I'm going to St Louis, Mr Sampson. That's cross state lines. The court done said –"

Aaron didn't have a chance. The blow came from nowhere. Laying there on the floor with blood spurting from his mouth, Aaron looked up at Mr Sampson, and he did another crazy thing: He grinned. Bull Sampson jumped up in the air and came down on Aaron with all his two hundred pounds. It made a crunchy sound. He jumped again, and the mob, maddened by the blood and heat, moved in to help him. They fell on Aaron like mad dogs. They beat him with chairs; they beat him with sticks; they beat him with guns.

Till this day, I don't know what come over me. The first thing I know I was running, and then I was standing in the middle of the white waiting room. Mr Sampson was the first to see me. He backed off, cocked his pistol, and said: "Booker, boy, you come one mo step and I'll kill you. What's a matter with you niggers today? All y'all gone crazy?"

"Please don't kill him," I begged. "You ain't got no call to treat him like that."

"So you saw it all, did you? Well, then, Booker, you musta saw the nigger preacher reach for my gun?"

"He didn't do that, Mr Sampson," I said. "He didn't –"

Mr Sampson put a big hairy hand on my tie and pulled me to him.

"Booker," he said sweetly. "You saw the nigger preacher reach for my gun, didn't you?"

I didn't open my mouth – I couldn't I was so scared – but I guess my eyes answered for me. Whatever Mr Sampson saw there musta convinced him 'cause he throwed me on the floor beside Aaron.

"Git this nigger out of here," he said, "and be quick about it."

Dropping to my knees, I put my hand on Aaron's chest; I didn't feel nothing. I felt his wrist; I didn't feel nothing. I got up and looked at them white folks with tears in my eyes. I looked at the women sitting crying on the benches. I looked at the men. I looked at Mr Sampson. I said, "He was a good man."

Mr Sampson said, "Move the nigger."

A big sigh came out of me, and I wrung my hands.

Mr Sampson said, "Move the nigger."

He grabbed my tie and twisted it, but I didn't feel nothing. My eyes were glued to his hands; there was blood under the fingernails, and the fingers – they looked like fat little red sausages. I screamed and Mr Sampson flung me down on the floor.

He said, "*Move the nigger.*"

I picked Aaron up and fixed his body over my shoulder and carried him outside. I sent for one of my boys, and we dressed him up and put him away real nice-like, and Rachel and the boy came and they cried and carried on, and yet somehow they seemed prouder of Aaron than ever before. And the coloured folks – they seemed proud, too. Crazy people. Didn't they know? Couldn't they see? It hadn't done no good. In fact, things got worse. The Northern newspapers started kicking up a stink, and Mr Rivers, the solicitor, announced they were going to hold a hearing. All of a sudden, Booker Taliaferro Brown became the biggest man in that town. My phone rang day and night: I got threats, I got promises, and I was offered bribes. Everywhere I turned somebody was waiting to ask me: "Whatcha gonna do? Whatcha gonna say?" To tell the truth, I didn't know myself. One day I would decide one thing, and the next day I would decide another.

It was Mr Rivers and Mr Sampson who called my attention to that. They came to my office one day and called me a shifty, no-good nigger. They said they expected me to stand by "my statement" in the train station that I saw Aaron reach for the gun. I hadn't said no such thing, but Mr Sampson said I said it, and he said he had witnesses who heard me say it. "And if you say anything else," he said, "I can't be responsible for your health. Now you know" – he put that bloody hand on my shoulder and he smiled his sweet death smile – "you *know* I wouldn't threaten you, but the boys" – he shook his head – "the boys are real worked up over this one."

It was long about then that I began to hate Aaron Lott. I'm ashamed to admit it now, but it's true: I hated him. He had lived his life; he had made his choice. Why should he live my life, too, and make me choose? It wasn't fair; it wasn't right; it wasn't Christian. What made me so mad was the fact that nothing I said would help Aaron. He was dead, and it wouldn't help one whit for me to say that he didn't reach for that gun. I tried to explain that to Rachel when she came to my office, moaning and crying, the night before the hearing.

"Listen to me, woman," I said. "Listen. Aaron was a good man. He lived a good life. He did a lot of good things, but he's *dead, dead, dead!* Nothing I say will bring him back. Bull Sampson's got ten niggers who are going to swear on a stack of Bibles that they saw Aaron reach for that gun. It won't do me or you or Aaron no good for me to swear otherwise."

What did I say that for? That woman liked to had a fit. She got down on her knees, and she begged me to go with Aaron.

"Go wit' him," she cried. "Booker. *Booker!* If you's a man, if you's a father, if you's a friend, go wit' Aaron."

That woman tore my heart up. I ain't never heard nobody beg like that.

"Tell the truth, Booker," she said. "That's all I'm asking. Tell the truth."

"Truth!" I said. "Hah! That's all you people talk about: truth. What do you know about truth? Truth is eating good and sleeping good. Truth is living, Rachel. Be loyal to the living."

Rachel backed off from me. You would have thought that I had cursed her or something. She didn't say nothing; she just stood there pressed against the door. She stood there saying nothing for so long that my nerves snapped.

"Say something," I shouted. "Say something – anything!"

She shook her head, slowly at first, and then her head started moving like it wasn't attached to her body. It went back and forth, back and forth, back and forth. I started toward her, but she jerked open the door and ran out into the night screaming.

That did it. I ran across the room to the filing cabinet, opened the bottom drawer, and took out a dusty bottle of Scotch. I started drinking, but the more I drank, the soberer I got. I guess I fell asleep 'cause I dreamed I buried Rachel and that everything went along fine until she jumped out of the casket and started screaming. I came awake with a start and knocked over the bottle. I reached for a rag and my hand stopped in mid-air.

"Of course," I said out loud and slammed my fist down on the Scotch-soaked papers.

I didn't see nothing.

Why didn't I think of it before?

I didn't see nothing.

Jumping up, I walked to and fro in the office. Would it work? I rehearsed it in my mind. All I could see was Aaron's back. I don't know whether he reached for the gun or not. All I know is that *for some reason* the men beat him to death.

Rehearsing the thing in my mind, I felt a great weight slip off my shoulders. I did a little jig in the middle of the floor and went upstairs to my bed, whistling. Sarah turned over and looked me up and down.

"What you happy about?"

"Can't a man be happy?" I asked.

She sniffed the air, said, "Oh," turned over, and mumbled something in her pillow. It came to me then for the first time that she was 'bout the only person in town who hadn't asked me what I was going to do. I thought about it for a little while, shrugged, and fell into bed with all my clothes on.

When I woke up the next morning, I had a terrible headache, and
my tongue was a piece of sandpaper. For a long while I couldn't
figure out what I was doing laying there with all my clothes on.
Then it came to me: this was the big day. I put on my black silk
suit, the one I wore for big funerals, and went downstairs to
breakfast. I walked into the dining room without looking and
bumped into Russell, the last person in the world I wanted to see.
He was my only child, but he didn't act like it. He was always
finding fault. He didn't like the way I talked to Negroes; he didn't
like the way I talked to white folks. He didn't like this; he didn't like
that. And to top it off, the young whippersnapper wanted to be an
artist. Undertaking wasn't good enough for him. He wanted to paint
pictures.

I sat down and grunted.

"Good morning, Papa." He said it like he meant it. He wants
something, I thought, looking him over closely, noticing that his
right eye was swollen.

"You been fighting again, boy?"

"Yes, Papa."

"You younguns. Education – that's what it is. Education! It's
ruining you."

He didn't say nothing. He just sat there, looking down when I
looked up and looking up when I looked down. This went on
through the grits and the eggs and the second cup of coffee.

"Whatcha looking at?" I asked.

"Nothing, Papa."

"Whatcha thinking?"

"Nothing, Papa."

"You lying, boy. It's written all over your face."

He didn't say nothing.

I dismissed him with a wave of my hand, picked up the paper, and
turned to the sports page.

"What are you going to do, Papa?"

The question caught me unawares. I know now that I was
expecting it, that I wanted him to ask it; but he put it so bluntly
that I was flabbergasted. I pretended I didn't understand.

"Do 'bout what, boy? Speak up!"

"About the trial, Papa."

I didn't say nothing for a long time. There wasn't much, in fact, I
could say; so I got mad.

"Questions, questions, questions," I shouted. "That's all I get in
this house – questions. You never have a civil word for your pa. I go

out of here and work my tail off, and you keep yourself shut up in that room of yours looking at them fool books, and now soon as your old man gets his back against the wall, you join the pack. I expected better than that of you, boy. A son ought to back his pa."

That hurt him. He picked up the coffeepot and poured himself another cup of coffee, and his hand trembled. He took a sip and watched me over the rim.

"They say you are going to chicken out, Papa."

"Chicken out? What that mean?"

"They're betting you'll 'Tom.'"

I leaned back in the chair and took a sip of coffee.

"So they're betting, huh?" The idea appealed to me. "Crazy people – they'd bet on a funeral."

I saw pain on his face. He sighed and said: "I bet, too, Papa."

The cup fell out my hand and broke, spilling black water over the tablecloth.

"You did what?"

"I bet you wouldn't 'Tom.'"

"You little fool." I fell out laughing, and then I stopped suddenly and looked at him closely. "How much you bet?"

"One hundred dollars."

I stood up.

"You're lying," I said. "Where'd you get that kind of money?"

"From Mamma."

"Sarah!" I shouted. "Sarah! You get in here. What kind of house you running, sneaking behind my back, giving this boy money to gamble with?"

Sarah leaned against the doorjamb. She was in her hot iron mood. There was no expression on her face. And her eyes were hard.

"I gave it to him, Booker," she said. "They called you an Uncle Tom. He got in a fight about it. He wanted to bet on you, Booker. *He* believes in you."

Suddenly I felt old and used up. I pulled a chair to me and sat down.

"Please," I said, waving my hand. "Please. Go away. Leave me alone. Please."

I sat there for maybe ten or fifteen minutes, thinking, praying. The phone rang. It was Mr Withers, the president of the bank. I had put in for a loan, and it had been turned down, but Mr Withers said there'd been a mistake, "New fellow, you know," he said, clucking his tongue. He said he knew that it was my lifelong dream to build a modern funeral home and to buy a Cadillac hearse. He said he sympathized with that dream, supported it, thought the town needed it, and thought I deserved it. "The loan will go through," he said. "Drop by and see me this morning after the hearing."

When I put that phone down, it was wet with sweat. I couldn't turn that new funeral home down, and Mr Withers knew it. My father had raised me on that dream, and before he died, he made me swear on a Bible, that I would make it good. And here it was on a platter, just for a word, a word that wouldn't hurt anybody.

I put on my hat and hurried to the courthouse. When they called my name, I walked in with my head held high. The courtroom was packed. The white folks had all the seats, and the coloured folks were standing in the rear. Whoever arranged the seating had set aside the first two rows for white men. They were sitting almost on top of each other, looking mean and uncomfortable in their best white shirts.

I walked up to the bench and swore on the Bible and took a seat. Mr Rivers gave me a little smile and waited for me to get myself set.

"State your name," he said.

"Booker Taliaferro Brown." I took a quick look at the first two rows and recognized at least ten of the men who killed Aaron.

"And your age?"

"Fifty-seven."

"You're an undertaker?"

"Yessir."

"You been living in this town all your life?"

"Yessir."

"You like it here, don't you, Booker?"

Was this a threat? I looked Mr Rivers in the face for the first time. He smiled.

I told the truth. I said, "Yessir."

"Now, calling your attention to the day of May 17th, did anything unusual happen on that day?"

The question threw me. I shook my head. Then it dawned on me. He was talking about –

"Yessir," I said. "That's the day Aaron got –" Something in Mr Rivers' face warned me, and I pulled up – "that's the day of the trouble at the train station."

Mr Rivers smiled. He looked like a trainer who'd just put a monkey through a new trick. You could feel the confidence and the contempt oozing out of him. I looked at his prissy little moustache and his smiling lips, and I got mad. Lifting my head a little bit, I looked him full in the eyes; I held the eyes for a moment, and I tried to tell the man behind the eyes that I was a man like him and that he didn't have no right to be using me and laughing about it. But he didn't get the message. The bastard – he chuckled softly, turned his back to me, and faced the audience.

"I believe you were with the preacher that day."

The water was getting deep. I scroonched down in my seat, closed the lids of my eyes, and looked dense.

"Yessir, Mr Rivers," I drawled. "Ah was."

"Now, Booker –" he turned around – "I believe you tried to keep the nigger preacher from getting out of line."

I hesitated. It wasn't a fair question. Finally, I said: "Yessir."

"You begged him not to go in the white side?"

"Yessir."

"And when that failed, you went over to *your* side – the *coloured* side – and looked through the window?"

"Yessir."

He put his hand in his coat pocket and studied my face.

"You saw *everything*, didn't you?"

"Just about." A muscle on the inside of my thigh started tingling.

Mr Rivers shuffled some papers he had in his hand. He seemed to be thinking real hard. I pushed myself against the back of the chair. Mr Rivers moved close, quick, and stabbed his finger into my chest.

"Booker, did you see the nigger preacher reach for Mr Sampson's gun?"

He backed away, smiling. I looked away from him, and I felt my heart trying to tear out of my skin. I looked out over the courtroom. It was still; wasn't even a fly moving. I looked at the white folks in front and the coloured folks in back, and I turned the question over in my mind. While I was doing that, waiting, taking my time, I noticed, out of the corner of my eye, that the smile on Mr Rivers' face was dying away. Suddenly, I had a terrible itch to know what that smile would turn into.

I said, "Nosir."

Mr Rivers stumbled backwards like he had been shot. Old Judge Sloan took off his glasses and pushed his head out over the bench. The whole courtroom seemed to be leaning in to me, and I saw Aaron's widow leaning back with her eyes closed, and it seemed to me at that distance that her lips were moving in prayer.

Mr Rivers was the first to recover. He put his smile back on, and he acted like my answer was in the script.

"You mean," he said, "that you didn't see it. It happened so quickly that you missed it?"

I looked at the bait, and I ain't gonna lie: I was tempted. He knew as well as I did what I meant, but he was gambling on my weakness. I had thrown away my funeral home, my hearse, everything I owned, and he was standing there like a magician, pulling them out of a hat, one at a time, dangling them, saying: "Looka here, looka here, don't they look pretty?" I was on top of a house, and he was betting that if he gave me a ladder I would come down. He was wrong, but you can't fault him for trying. He hadn't never met no black man who would go all the way. I looked him in the eye and went the last mile.

"Aaron didn't reach for that gun," I said. "Them people, they just fell on —"

"Hold it," he shouted. "I want to remind you that there are laws in this state against perjury. You can go to jail for five years for what you just said. Now I know you've been conferring with those NAACP fellows, but I want to remind you of the statements you made to Sheriff Sampson and me. Judge —" he dismissed me with a wave of his hand — "Judge, this *man* —" he caught himself and it was my turn to smile — "this *boy* is lying. Ten niggers have testified that they saw the preacher reach for the gun. Twenty white people saw it. You've heard their testimony. I want to withdraw this witness, and I want to reserve the right to file perjury charges against him."

Judge Sloan nodded. He pushed his bottom lip over his top one. "You can step down," he said. "I want to warn you that perjury is a very grave offence. You —"

"Judge, I didn't —"

"Nigger!" He banged his gavel. "Don't you interrupt me. Now git out of here."

Two guards pushed me outside and waved away the reporters. Billy Giles, Mr Sampson's assistant, came out and told me Mr Sampson wanted me out of town before sundown. "And he says you'd better get out before the Northern reporters leave. He won't be responsible for your safety after that."

I nodded and went on down the stairs and started out the door.

"Booker!"

Rachel and a whole line of Negroes were running down the stairs. I stepped outside and waited for them. Rachel ran up and throwed her arms around me. "It don't take but one, Booker," she said. "It don't take but one." Somebody else said: "They whitewashed it, they whitewashed it, but you spoiled it for 'em."

Russell came out then and stood over to the side while the others

crowded around to shake my hands. Then the others sensed that he
was waiting, and they made a little aisle. He walked up to me kind
of slow-like and he said, "Thank you, sir." That was the first time in
his whole seventeen years that that boy had said "sir" to me. I
cleared my throat, and when I opened my eyes, Sarah was standing
beside me. She didn't say nothing; she just put her hand in mine
and stood there. It was long about then, I guess, when I realized
that I wasn't seeing so good. They say I cried, but I don't believe a
word of it. It was such a hot day and the sun was shining so bright
that the sweat rolling down my face blinded me. I wiped the sweat
out of my eyes, and some more people came up and said a lot of
foolish things about me showing the white folks and following in
Aaron's footsteps. I wasn't doing no such fool thing. Ol' Man Rivers
just put the thing to me in a way it hadn't been put before – man to
man. It was simple, really. Any man would have done it.

Follow-up

1   Aaron Lott knows that in going through the white waiting
    room he is risking his life. When trying to dissuade him, the
    narrator tells him to think of the son he would leave behind. But
    it is the thought of his son that pushes Aaron on. How and why
    is he risking his life for his son?
2   *(a)* What does Booker, the narrator, think of Aaron's plan to defy
        the racial barriers?
    (b) Why, when Aaron is dead, does Booker come to hate him?
3   Give a detailed account of why Booker decides, in the
    courtroom, to tell the truth.
4   What is significant about the last sentence of the story, "Any
    man would have done it"?
5   Write a story in which the hero or heroine has to make a
    decision that will affect everything that happens in his or her life
    from that moment on. It might, for instance, be a decision to
    marry someone of a different race, or to join a particular
    organization, or to give up comfort for a more harshly disciplined
    life.

Soledad Brother

from *The Prison Letters of George Jackson*, 1970

*George Jackson died in prison in 1971. He had been in prison since
1960. Then, at the age of eighteen, he had been advised by his
lawyer to plead guilty to robbery charges. His lawyer told him that
such a plea would result in a lighter sentence. He had stolen seventy
dollars from a petrol station and he was given an indeterminate
sentence of "one year to life". Each year his case would be reviewed
by the parole board.*

*In prison he developed a powerful, revolutionary political
consciousness that was never acceptable to the parole board and he
remained in prison for the rest of his life.*

*In 1970 he was charged with the murder of a prison guard in
Soledad Prison. In August 1970 his brother Jonathan, then just
seventeen, invaded single-handed the San Rafael courthouse where
George was being tried; he armed George and the two convicts
charged with him and took five hostages. As he left the courtroom he
shouted "free the Soledad brothers". Within minutes Jonathan was
dead.*

*George Jackson became a symbol for the fight against oppression.
He died in a prison riot in August 1971. While he was in prison a
book of his letters to his friends and relatives was published. A small
selection of these letters is included below. They are a moving
testament to his courage and his intellect.*

March 30th, 1965

Dear Father,

 I haven't read anything or studied in a week now. I have been
devoting all my time to thought. I trust you are all in health. I think
of my personal past quite often. This is uncomfortable sometimes
but necessary. I try not to let my past mistakes bother me too much,
though some seem almost unpardonable. If it were not for the few
intermixed little victories, my confidence in my ability would be
irreparably shaken.

 Though I know I am a victim of social injustice and economic
pressure and though I understand the forces that work to drive so
many of our kind to places like this and to mental institutions, I can't
help but know that I proceeded wrong somewhere. I could have

done a lot worse. You know our people react in different ways to this neoslavery, some just give in completely and join the other side. They join some christian cult and cry out for integration. These are the ones who doubt themselves most. They are the weakest and hardest to reach with the new doctrine. Some become inveterate drinkers and narcotic users in an attempt to gain some mental solace for the physical depravity they suffer. I've heard them say, "There's no hope without dope." Some hire on as a janitor, bellboy, redcap, cook, elevator boy, singer, boxer, baseball player, or maybe a freak at some sideshow and pretend that all is as well as is possible. They think since it's always been this way it must always remain this way; these are the fatalists, they serve and entertain and rationalize.

Then there are those who resist and rebel but do not know what, who, why, or how exactly they should go about this. They are aware but confused. They are the least fortunate, for they end where I have ended. By using half measures and failing dismally to effect any real improvement in their condition, they fall victim to the full fury and might of the system's repressive agencies. Believe me, every dirty trick of deception and brutality is employed without shame, without honour, without humanity, without reservation to either convert or destroy a rebellious arm. Believe me, when I say that I begin to weary of the sun. I am by nature a gentle man, I love the simple things of life, good food, good wine, an expressive book, music, pretty black women. I used to find enjoyment in a walk in the rain, summer evenings in a place like Harrisburg. Remember how I used to love Harrisburg. All of this is gone from me, all the gentle, shy characteristics of the black men have been wrung unceremoniously from my soul. The buffets and blows of this have and have-not society have engendered in me a flame that will live, will live to grow, until it either destroys my tormentor or myself. You don't understand this but I must say it. Maybe when you remember this ten or twenty years from now you'll comprehend. I don't think of life in the same sense that you or most black men of your generation think of it, it is not important to me how long I live, I think only of how I live, how well, how nobly. We think if we are to be men again we must stop working for nothing, competing against each other for the little they allow us to possess, stop selling our women or allowing them to be used and handled against their will, stop letting our children be educated by the barbarian, using their language, dress, and customs, and most assuredly stop turning our cheeks.

GEORGE

July 1965

Dear Father,

Well I guess you know that I'm aware that this is not the best of all
possible lives. You also know that I thank you for trying to cushion the
shocks and strains that history has made it our lot to have to endure.
But the make-believe game has ended now. I don't think it necessary
for me to burden myself with listing strains we've endured. You are
intelligent enough to know. At each phase of this long train of
tyrannies, we have conducted ourselves in a very meek and civilized
manner, with only polite pleas for justice and moderation, all to no
avail. We have shown a noble indisposition to react with the passion
that each new oppression engenders. But any fool should be able to
see that this cannot be allowed to continue. Any fool should be able to
see that nature allows no such imbalances as this to exist for long. We
have petitioned for judicial redress. We have remonstrated, supplicated,
demonstrated, and prostrated ourselves before the feet of our self-
appointed administrators. We have done all that we can do to
circumvent the eruption that now comes on apace. The point of no
return in our relationship has long been passed. I know what must
and will take place so I follow my ends through to the most glorious
conclusion. Don't make me waste my time and energy winning you to
a position that you should already support with all your sympathies.
The same forces that have made your life miserable, the same forces
that have made your life senseless and unrewarding, threaten me and
all our posterity. I know the way out. If you cannot help, sit back and
listen, watch. You are charged with the responsibility of acknowledging
the truth, my friend, and supporting it with whatever means, no
matter how humble, are in your power. I am charged to right the
wrong, lift the burden from the backs of future generations. I will not
shrink from my duties. I will never falter or waver before the task, but
we will go forward – to resolve this conflict once and forever. Of all
the twenty thousand known years of advanced civilization, the years
that are now coming on will be the most momentous.

GEORGE

February 1st, 1967

Dear Mother,

Things are normal here, the usual turmoil. I hope you are well. I
hope you are doing enough light exercise each day to work up some
perspiration and not eating the wrong things – pork, sugar, white

bread, etc. I'm very careful in this respect and enjoy almost perfect
health and great reserves of energy and strength in spite of my
circumstances. But I do heavy exercises, maybe two hours' worth a
day, every day. In close confinement where I cannot get to any
workout facilities, as now, I work out somewhat differently. I take
neat piles of books and magazines tied together and exercise with
them. For you I imagine some deep knee bends, touch your toes,
and say some push-ups would be fine. You would do five sets
of ten of each exercise. For example, start by doing ten push-ups,
rest a minute or two, do ten more, rest a few minutes, etc.,
until you get to five sets, then go to the next exercise. Stay young
and firm that way. Resistance to bodily disorders stays high, or
builds up.

You know when they locked me up this time all my personal
property came up missing. I'll have to replace everything – two
personal chess sets, toilet articles, the black sweat shirts. I had four
of these but saved only the one I had on. Even the plastic tumblers I
used to drink with in the cell, everything is gone. I'm not sure about
the typewriter, I can't get any information on it. I know that I don't
have it here; whether it is safe somewhere else I don't know. Then,
too, several of us blacks were locked up at the same time for just
about the same thing. They go to the small adjustment centre yard
each day for two hours; I am forced to remain in my cell, no fresh
air, no sun, twenty-four hours a day in here. It doesn't bother me,
though. I've trained myself not to be disorganized by any measure
they take against me. I exercise in here, and pursue my studies. That
fills my day out nicely. Since I know that I am the original man and
will soon inherit this earth, I am content to just prepare myself and
wait, nothing can stop me now! But I do sometimes wonder just
exactly how they got the way they are. I know beyond question the
extent of the evil that lurks in their hearts; I see the *insane* passion,
inherent in their characters, to dominate all that they come in
contact with. What aggressive psychosis impels a man to want his
dessert and mine too, to want to feast at every table, to want to cast
his shadow over every land? I don't know what they are; some folks
call them devils (doers of evil). I don't know if this is an adequate
description. It goes much deeper. From their footprints I see that
they are descendants of *Pithecanthropus erectus* like ourselves, but
here the similarity ends. I refuse to compare myself with a man who
for one truth will tell ninety-nine lies; with a vampire who cannot
stand in the sun and do a day's work; and with someone who
thrives upon the blood, sweat, and tears of any who fall within his

power, But doomsday is dawning; on this most awesome day all imbalances and contradictions must be resolved, and it will be some of us who will be left to rebuild this world and people these lands with civil men.

GEORGE

Follow-up

1   What connection is there between the letter from son to father of July 1965, and the tensions in the father and son relationship of the story *The Convert*?
2   From the letter 1 February 1967, what do you learn about:
    (a) George Jackson's personal discipline?
    (b) the depth of his hatred?
3   From all the letters, what picture do you begin to build of George Jackson's character and beliefs?
4   Write a letter home to your parents from a prison cell. Imagine you have been the victim of a severe injustice, and must spend years in prison either because of a wrongful conviction or because you committed a crime in circumstances in which you felt you had no choice.

The Seven Days

from *Song of Solomon* by Toni Morrison, 1977

Song of Solomon *is a beautiful and powerful novel. It deals with the parallel lives of Macon Dead Jr. and his friend Guitar Bains. Macon, known as Milkman, is the son of a wealthy black property owner whose approach to life is dilettante. Guitar, not cushioned by money, sees life in harsher terms.*

Milkman realizes that a distance has come between them and in the extract that follows he pushes Guitar to reveal a secret and terrifying side of his life. Guitar sees the way of fighting back in cold and ruthless terms.

"We've been friends a long time, Guitar. There's nothing you don't know about me. I can tell you anything – whatever our differences, I know I can trust you. But for some time now it's been a one-way street. You know what I mean? I talk to you, but you don't talk to me. You don't think I can be trusted?"

"I don't know if you can or not."

"Try me."

"I can't. Other people are involved."

"Then don't tell me about other people; tell me about you."

Guitar looked at him for a long time. Maybe, he thought. Maybe I can trust you. Maybe not, but I'll risk it anyway because one day . . .

"Okay," he said aloud, "but you have to know that what I tell you can't go any further. And if it does, you'll be dropping a rope around my neck. Now do you still want to know it?"

"Yeah."

"You sure?"

"I'm sure."

Guitar poured some more hot water over his tea. He looked into his cup for a minute while the leaves settled slowly to the bottom. "I suppose you know that white people kill black people from time to time, and most folks shake their heads and say, 'Eh, eh, eh, ain't that a shame?'"

Milkman raised his eyebrows. He thought Guitar was going to let him in on some deal he had going. But he was slipping into his race bag. He was speaking slowly, as though each word had to count, and as though he were listening carefully to his own words. "I can't suck my teeth or say 'Eh, eh, eh.' I had to do something. And the only thing left to do is balance it; keep things on an even keel. Any man, any woman, or any child is good for five to seven generations of heirs before they're bred out. So every death is the death of five to seven generations. You can't stop them from killing us, from trying to get rid of us. And each time they succeed, they get rid of five to seven generations. I help keep the numbers the same.

"There is a society. It's made up of a few men who are willing to take some risks. They don't initiate anything; they don't even choose. They are as indifferent as rain. But when a Negro child, Negro woman, or Negro man is killed by whites and nothing is done about it by *their* courts, this society selects a similar victim at random, and they execute him or her in a similar manner if they can. If the Negro was hanged, they hang; if a Negro was burnt, they burn; raped and murdered, they rape and murder. If they can. If they can't do it precisely in the same manner, they do it any way they can, but they do it. They call themselves the Seven Days. They are made up of seven men. Always seven and only seven. If one of them dies or leaves or is no longer effective, another is chosen. Not right away, because that kind of choosing takes time. But they don't seem to be in a hurry. Their secret is time. To take the time, to last. Not to grow; that's dangerous because you might become known. They don't write their names in toilet stalls or brag to women. Time and silence. Those are their weapons, and they go on forever.

"It got started in 1920, when that private from Georgia was killed after his balls were cut off and after that veteran was blinded when he came home from France in World War I. And it's been operating ever since. I am one of them now."

Milkman had held himself very still all the time Guitar spoke. Now he felt tight, shrivelled, and cold.

"You? You're going to kill people?"

"Not people. White people?"

"But why?"

"I just told you. It's necessary; it's got to be done. To keep the ratio the same."

"And if it isn't done? If it just goes on the way it has?"

"Then the world is a zoo, and I can't live in it."

"Why don't you just hunt down the ones who did the killing? Why kill innocent people? Why not just those who did it?"

"It doesn't matter who did it. Each and every one of them could do it. So you just get any one of them. There are no innocent white people, because every one of them is a potential nigger-killer, if not an actual one. You think Hitler surprised them? You think just because they went to war they thought he was a freak? Hitler's the most natural white man in the world. He killed Jews and Gypsies because he didn't have us. Can you see those Klansmen shocked by him? No, you can't."

"But people who lynch and slice off people's balls – they're crazy, Guitar, crazy."

"Every time somebody does a thing like that to one of us, they say the people who did it were crazy or ignorant. That's like saying they were drunk. Or constipated. Why isn't cutting a man's eyes out, cutting his nuts off, the kind of thing you never get too drunk or ignorant to do? Too crazy to do? Too constipated to do? And more to the point, how come Negroes, the craziest, most ignorant people in America, don't get that crazy and that ignorant? No. White people are unnatural. As a race they are unnatural. And it takes a strong effort of the will to overcome an unnatural enemy."

"What about the nice ones? Some whites made sacrifices for Negroes. Real sacrifices."

"That just means there are one or two natural ones. But they haven't been able to stop the killing either. They are outraged, but that doesn't stop it. They might even speak out, but that doesn't stop it either. They might even inconvenience themselves, but the killing goes on and on. So will we."

"You're missing the point. There're not just one or two. There're a lot."

"Are there? Milkman, if Kennedy got drunk and bored and was sitting around a potbellied stove in Mississippi, he might join a lynching party just for the hell of it. Under those circumstances his unnaturalness would surface. But I know I wouldn't join one no matter how drunk I was or how bored, and I know you wouldn't either, nor any black man I know or ever heard tell of. Ever. In any world, at any time, just get up and go find somebody white to slice up. But they *can* do it. And they don't even do it for profit, which is why they do most things. They do it for fun. Unnatural."

"What about . . ." Milkman searched his memory for some white person who had shown himself unequivocally supportive of Negroes. "Schweitzer. Albert Schweitzer. Would he do it?"

"In a minute. He didn't care anything about those Africans. They could have been rats. He was in a laboratory testing *himself* – proving he could work on human dogs."

"What about Eleanor Roosevelt?"

"I don't know about the women. I can't say what their women would do, but I do remember the picture of those white mothers holding up their babies so they could get a look at some black men burning on a tree. So I have my suspicions about Eleanor Roosevelt. But *none* about Mr Roosevelt. You could've taken him and his wheelchair and put him in a small dusty town in Alabama and given him some tobacco, a checkerboard, some whiskey, and a rope and he'd have done it too. What I'm saying is, under certain conditions they would *all* do it. And under the same circumstances we would not. So it doesn't matter that some of them *haven't* done it. I listen. I read. And now I know that they know it too. They know they are unnatural. Their writers and artists have been saying it for years. Telling them they are unnatural, telling them they are depraved. They call it tragedy. In the movies they call it adventure. It's just depravity that they try to make glorious, natural. But it

ain't. The disease they have is in their blood, in the structure of
their chromosomes.''

"You can prove this, I guess. Scientifically?"

"No."

"Shouldn't you be able to prove it before you act on something
like that?"

"Did they prove anything scientifically about us before they killed
us? No. They killed us first and then tried to get some scientific
proof about why we should die."

"Wait a minute, Guitar. If they are as bad, as unnatural, as you
say, why do you want to be like them? Don't you want to be better
than they are?"

"I am better."

"But now you're doing what the worst of them do."

"Yes, but I am reasonable."

"Reasonable? How?"

"I am not, one, having fun, two, trying to gain power or public
attention or money or land; three, angry at anybody."

"You're not angry? You must be!"

"Not at all. I hate doing it. I'm afraid to do it. It's hard to do it
when you aren't angry or drunk or doped up or don't have a
personal grudge against the person."

"I can't see how it helps. I can't see how it helps anybody."

"I told you. Numbers. Balance. Ratio. And the earth, the
land."

"I'm not understanding you."

"The earth is soggy with black people's blood. And before us
Indian blood. Nothing can cure them, and if it keeps on there won't
be any of us left and there won't be any land for those who are left.
So the numbers have to remain static."

"But there are more of them than us."

"Only in the West. But still the ratio can't widen in their favour."

"But you should want everybody to know that the society exists.
Then maybe that would help stop it. What's the secrecy for?"

"To keep from getting caught."

"Can't you even let other Negroes know about it? I mean to give
us hope?"

"No."

"Why not?"

"Betrayal. The possibility of betrayal."

"Well, let *them* know. Let white people know. Like the Mafia or
the Klan; frighten them into behaving."

"You're talking foolishness. How can you let one group know and not the other? Besides, we are not like them. The Mafia is unnatural. So is the Klan. One kills for money, the other kills for fun. And they have huge profits and protection at their disposal. We don't. But it's not about other people knowing. We don't even tell the victims. We just whisper to him, 'Your Day has come.' The beauty of what we do is its secrecy, its smallness. The fact that nobody needs the unnatural satisfaction of talking about it. Telling about it. We don't discuss it among ourselves, the details. We just get an assignment. If the Negro was killed on a Wednesday, the Wednesday man takes it; if he was killed on Monday, the Monday man takes that one. And we just notify one another when it's completed, not how or who. And if it ever gets to be too much, like it was for Robert Smith, we do *that* rather than crack and tell somebody. Like Porter. It was getting him down. They thought somebody would have to take over his day. He just needed a rest and he's okay now."

Milkman stared at his friend and then let the spasm he had been holding back run through him. "I can't buy it, Guitar."

"I know that."

"There's too much wrong with it."

"Tell me."

"Well, for one thing, you'll get caught eventually."

"Maybe. But if I'm caught I'll just die earlier than I'm supposed to – not better than I'm supposed to. And how I die or when doesn't interest me. What I die *for* does. It's the same as what I live for. Besides, if I'm caught they'll accuse me and kill me for one crime, maybe two, never for all. And there are still six other days in the week. We've been around for a long long time. And believe me, we'll be around for a long long time to come."

"You can't marry."

"No."

"Have children."

"No."

"What kind of life is that?"

"Very satisfying."

"There's no love in it."

"No love? No love? Didn't you hear me? What I'm doing ain't about hating white people. It's about loving us. Above loving you. My whole life is love."

"Man, you're confused."

"Am I? When those concentration camp Jews hunt down Nazis, are they hating Nazis or loving dead Jews?"

"It's not the same thing."

"Only because they have money and publicity."

"No; because they turn them over to the courts. You kill and you don't kill the killers. You kill innocent people."

"I told you there are no –"

"And you don't correct a thing by –"

"We poor people, Milkman. I work at an auto plant. The rest of us barely eke out a living. Where's the money, the state, the country to finance our justice? You say Jews try their catches in a court. Do we have a court? Is there one courthouse in one city in the country where a jury would convict them? There are places right now where a Negro still can't testify against a white man. Where the judge, the jury, the court, are legally bound to ignore anything a Negro has to say. What that means is that a black man is a victim of a crime only when a white man says he is. Only then. If there was anything like or near justice or courts when a cracker kills a Negro, there wouldn't have to be no Seven Days. But there ain't; so we are. And we do it without money, without support, without costumes, without newspapers, without senators, without lobbyists, and without illusions!"

"You sound like that red-headed Negro named X. Why don't you join him and call yourself Guitar X?"

"X, Bains – what difference does it make? I don't give a damn about names."

"You miss his point. His point is to let white people know you don't accept your slave name."

"I don't give a shit what white people know or even think. Besides, I do accept it. It's part of who I am. Guitar is *my* name. Bains is the slave master's name. And I'm all of that. Slave names don't bother me; but slave status does."

"And knocking off white folks changes your slave status?"

"Believe it."

"Does it do anything for my slave status?"

Guitar smiled. "Well, doesn't it?"

"Hell, no." Milkman frowned. "Am I going to live any longer because you all read the newspaper and then ambush some poor old white man?"

"It's not about you living longer. It's about how you live and why It's about whether your children can make other children. It's about trying to make a world where one day white people will think before they lynch."

"Guitar, none of that shit is going to change how I live or how

any other Negro lives. What you're doing is crazy. And something
else: it's a habit. If you do it enough, you can do it to anybody.
You know what I mean? A torpedo is a torpedo, I don't care what
his reasons. You can off any body you don't like. You can off
me."

"We don't off Negroes."

"You hear what you said? *Negroes.* Not Milkman. Not 'No, I can't
touch *you*, Milkman,' but 'We don't off Negroes.' Shit, man, suppose
you all change your parliamentary rules?"

"The Days are the Days. It's been that way for a long time."

Milkman thought about that. "Any other young dudes in it? Are
all the others older? You the only young one?"

"Why?"

"Cause young dudes are subject to change the rules."

"You worried about yourself, Milkman?" Guitar looked amused.

"No. Not really." Milkman put his cigarette out and reached for
another one. "Tell me, what's your day?"

"Sunday. I'm the Sunday man."

Milkman rubbed the ankle of his short leg. "I'm scared for you,
man."

"That's funny. I'm scared for you too."

Follow-up

1   Looking at the whole extract, what justifications does Guitar
    give for the aims and methods of the Seven Days?
2   What arguments does Milkman use to counter him?
3   What do you think of the arguments that Guitar uses?
4   Write a scene from a play in which two people hold another as a
    political hostage. The two have demanded that all prisoners who
    hold the same political beliefs as they do be freed from jail. If
    this does not happen by the deadline they have set they have
    promised to kill the hostage.
        Write the scene when the deadline is up and the execution has
    to take place. One of the two has built up some kind of human
    bond with the prisoner; this leads to heated arguments and
    difficult decisions.